AMAZING JOB SEARCH GAMEPLAN

A Beginner's Guide to Getting the Job You'll Love

by
Richard Blazevich

Amazing Job Skills Publishing Company
Dallas, Texas
www.amazingjobskills.com

Acknowledgements

I'd like to thank my lovely wife, who gave me the idea for this book and encouraged me throughout the writing process. She's also been incredibly supportive while I traveled around the country as a corporate recruiter over the years.

I'd also like to thank my twelve-year-old daughter. She provided the first round of proofreading for my books at very reasonable rates. Hopefully, some of the tips from my books will stick with her, and she'll be able to impress employment recruiters someday as a result.

I'm also thankful for Eric Bishop, my co-author for my first book. He introduced me to many tools that have been invaluable in the book writing process.

INTRODUCTION

Contents

INTRODUCTION

Introduction

Over the past twenty years, I've interviewed hundreds of job candidates. Most of them were bright and highly motivated. Very few of them had the interview skills needed to get the jobs they wanted.

In rare instances, I've interviewed candidates who were amazing. They had a compelling answer to every question they were asked, and they received offers from nearly every recruiter who interviewed them.

If you want to become one of these superstar job candidates, this book is for you. You'll find a game plan for dazzling recruiters, along with incredible answers to even the toughest interview questions. You'll find tips for researching companies and figuring out exactly what recruiters are looking for. You'll also receive advice on refining your skills and using resources that are available to you for free.

I used many of the techniques in this book when job hunting. When I first entered business school, my fellow students might have elected me "Least Likely to Succeed" (if my school had such an award). I was awkward. I had no experience in my chosen career field. Yet, by the time I finished my two-year program, I had an internship at one of the best marketing companies in the world. I also received job offers from several powerhouse companies, including Frito-Lay, General Mills, Kraft, SC Johnson, and Quaker.

These impressive results didn't happen because I was talented. My natural ability paled in comparison to that of my fellow students. They happened because I learned the secrets to interviewing. This book will reveal those secrets to you.

When you were in school, you might have spent years getting an education in your chosen subject matter. However, you may have received very little help in getting the types of jobs you wanted.

When I was in school, I was lucky enough to receive life-changing advice from my school's career counselors. Their coaching set me up for years of success in my career. Now, I use the techniques I learned in school to coach people on how to get the jobs they really want.

After I graduated, I started recruiting people for my company's marketing department. I noticed that many of the most accomplished candidates didn't know how to answer interview questions. Their responses were often vague and didn't communicate their true potential. I knew that without strong interview skills, they would never make it through our rigorous selection process.

When I found particularly talented candidates who performed poorly during interviews, I offered them suggestions to improve their skills. Next, I began organizing interview workshops for student organizations and career development offices at the schools where my company recruited.

I've also helped many friends and family members with their job hunting. Career coaching is my passion. I'm excited to share my techniques with you.

This book represents the playbook I developed for my interview preparation workshops. My hope is that you can learn from my approach so that you'll be able to get the interviews you want. Then, you'll nail those interviews using the skills you've developed from the processes described within these pages.

To illustrate some of the concepts, I've included a story about a fictional job hunter who became successful at interviewing. While this specific person doesn't exist in the real world, she represents the combined experiences of many people I've coached over the years.

In each chapter, I'll summarize the key lessons from the story. I'll also provide tools and templates you can use to dramatically improve the skills you need to receive job offers.

If you've read my other book, *Amazing Interview Answers*, you'll notice that some of the content is repeated in this book. Please forgive the duplication. You'll find that most of the content in this book is new. I suggest that you read this book first to build your strategy. Then, as you practice your answers to interview questions, use *Amazing Interview Answers* to help refine your own amazing answers to the most commonly asked interview questions.

Also, I have a version of this book that is written for college students. It's called *Amazing Job Search Gameplan, College Student Edition*. If you know a student who will be entering the job market soon, please encourage them to read the student version. It includes most of the content in this book, plus additional information about resources available specifically to help college students find their dream jobs.

Now, let's get started.

1. Build Your Strategy

The first step in your job-hunting journey will be to create your strategy. Like any strategy, this involves defining your goals, identifying your options, and making the best choices to get the results you want.

Start by spending some time looking over a variety of job descriptions that might interest you, just to make sure you're on the right path. Unfortunately, most of us were never required to understand job duties before selecting our career direction. Some of us might have taken classes in school that provided some idea of what's involved in our future careers, but many of us didn't.

This lack of preparation can have disastrous results. For example, I started my career in accounting, which was absolutely the wrong choice for me. I chose the field because I enjoyed business and I wanted job security. While accounting met those two criteria, if I had taken the time to read any job description for an accountant, I would have heard sirens going off in my head telling me to avoid that career. Instead, I spent years in accounting jobs that made me miserable.

A typical accounting job description includes words like *organize, verify,* and *audit.* These are all things I hate doing. If I had read through a few other job descriptions, I might have stumbled across my real calling, which is marketing. I might have found a job description with words like *create, develop,* and *lead.* These are the very things I love doing.

There's actually an outstanding government website with hundreds of useful job descriptions. Yes, you read that right – an outstanding government website! Who would have thought?

I recommend that you spend a few minutes on the U.S. government's site for the Bureau of Labor Statistics. The website address is www.bls.gov/ooh. OOH stands for Occupational Outlook Handbook. I know it may sound incredibly boring, and while I freely admit that it's not the most entertaining site in the world, the content is extremely helpful. Our goal, after all, is not exactly entertainment, is it? Our goal is to find the information we need to get the jobs we want.

On the site, you will find job descriptions for hundreds of careers. If the duties for your chosen career field get you excited, that's a good sign. If they make you cringe, start searching for other options. You might be in the right general area, like how business was the right area for me, but you might be looking at the wrong specific job, like how accounting was wrong for me.

If nothing in your chosen career field gets you excited, that's OK. You may be in the wrong field. It's better to figure that out now than to do so after you've spent years struggling in a job you don't enjoy.

Hopefully, once you've spent some time browsing around the Occupational Outlook Handbook, you'll find a job description that gets you excited, or at least puts a smile on your face. Once you find the type of job you want, it will be time to plan your strategy.

The next step is setting your goal. That should be easy. Your goal could be to get a good job with a great company in your preferred line of work.

Before you jump into the search process, I recommend that you define the criteria for the job you want. You should write a list of things that are most important to you. That list could include geographic location, company culture, pay range, a flexible work schedule, or any other elements that you consider important.

Now it's time to define your options. That might take a little longer. It will involve finding target companies for your job hunt. The internet is full of resources to help you do this. I recommend starting with popular job sites like CareerBuilder, Job.com, Indeed, and Monster.

On those sites, you can find hundreds of listings for jobs near you. You'll also find the most valuable tools for your job search process, which are job descriptions for specific jobs. I cannot emphasize enough the importance of job descriptions. They are your secret weapons against the other candidates competing with you for jobs you want. Later in this book, I'll explain how to use job descriptions to learn exactly what employers want to see from candidates.

So, let's find a few potential jobs. Spend a few hours browsing through those job sites to see what's available in your area. In the first few minutes on each site, you should be able to pull up job listings in your chosen career field.

When you find a job that looks interesting, enter it onto your Job Hunting Tracker. What's a Job Hunting Tracker? It's a list of jobs you might want to apply for.

If you're a paper-and-pencil person, feel free to use the Job Strategy Template located in the Reference Materials section near the back of this book, or grab a notebook and start building your tracker there. If you're a computer person, use Microsoft Excel, Notability, or whatever program or app you prefer for keeping notes.

On your tracker, include the following information about each potential job:

- company name
- job title
- listing location (job site) or recruiter contact info
- job description, key duties, & qualifications
- comments
- date you'll submit an application or resume

I recommend that you also copy and save the job description into a folder where you can find it later.

In addition to searching for jobs online, don't forget to ask your friends, family members, and anyone else you're comfortable with if they know of any available jobs in your chosen field. Some of them may know about great opportunities.

Using a job tracker is the best way to organize your job search. It will not only focus your attention, but also give you a sense of accomplishment. As you record potential employers and send out your resumes, you'll see that you're making progress toward your objective of finding your dream job.

Let's see how this approach works in practical terms as we read a fictional story about a person who is coming to terms with being in the wrong job.

Lisa and Sandy
Part 1

Lisa sat in her cubicle, staring at her monitor. It must be almost time for lunch. She glanced at her watch: 10:00 a.m. She had only been at work for an hour. There were still two more hours to go until her lunch break. How could that be? It seemed like she had been working in her cubicle all morning. A commonly occurring thought popped into her head: *I hate my job.*

"Lisa…Lisa…are you there?" It was Sandy's voice coming from the other side of Lisa's cubicle wall. Sandy was one of the other bookkeepers in her department. While she must have been ten years older than Lisa, she seemed five years younger. She was always so cheerful. Lisa hated that about Sandy.

"Lisa, are you gonna have the weekly tracker ready for our meeting this afternoon?"

"Crap," Lisa thought. "I haven't even started the tracker." It was a report she easily could do in her sleep. If she could stay focused, it might take her an hour to complete. But most weeks, it took her half a day. It wasn't that it was difficult. It was just so, well, dull.

Lisa sat up straight. "Yeah, I'll have it in time for the meeting." She started typing on her keyboard. An hour later, Lisa was staring at her computer again, with the weekly tracker less than half done. The ever-recurring thought popped back into her head: "*I hate my job.*"

Sandy stepped into Lisa's cubicle. "Hey, Lisa, are you doing anything interesting this weekend?"

"I don't know if I'd call it interesting. I'm spending time at my parents' house. My sister'll be there. My mom and I are gonna help with planning her wedding. How 'bout you?"

"I'm looking for something to do. My husband is going on golf trip with his buddies, and my kids are at camp this month."

Without even thinking, Lisa heard herself say, "You're welcome to come with me. I've got a two-hour drive to my parents' house, and I could use the company."

Sandy paused. "Oh, I don't know. I don't want to impose on your family time."

"It's no imposition. My parents have a big house, and they love having company. They keep bugging me to bring friends when I visit. Come on. It'll be fun."

"Well, if you don't mind. When do we leave?"

That Saturday morning, Lisa picked up Sandy at her charming, suburban house. After half an hour of small talk, Sandy asked, "Lisa, if you don't mind me asking, do you like what you're doing?"

"I don't mind it. Driving isn't my favorite thing, but it is nice having you here keeping me company."

Sandy shook her head. "No, that's not what I meant. Do you like your job?"

"Why do you ask?"

"Well, you're really smart. And I know you can do the work. Sometimes, it seems like you don't really enjoy it."

"Nobody enjoys their job."

"I do. At least, I do now. I used to hate what I did, but now, I really like it."

"Really? What changed?"

"My job. I used to be in marketing. I hated it. I was good at it, but it just wasn't for me."

Lisa was confused. "You hated marketing, and you like bookkeeping? That doesn't make any sense. I'd kill for a marketing job."

"Marketing isn't for everyone. It was too unpredictable for me. I like consistency. I like routine. With marketing, I never knew what I'd be doing each day. I hated that part in particular."

"Ugh! I hate routine. That's the worst part of my job. It drives me crazy."

"So why do you like bookkeeping?"

Lisa thought for a moment. "Nothing. It's just a job, a paycheck. And it beats working at my parents' diner. If I didn't have my bookkeeping job, I'd have to move back to my hometown and work for them."

"You know you have other options. I used to feel trapped in my marketing job. That was, until I got fed up and found a job I really like."

"Really? How did that happen?"

"In one of my annual performance reviews, my boss told me I had more ability than other people at my level, but I wasn't getting good results. That hit me hard.

I spent the next several weeks in a funk. Then, I started thinking about what I liked about the job and what I didn't.

"I liked the business stuff. I've always enjoyed working with numbers. But I didn't like the creative stuff. So, I started thinking about other jobs I might like. I do this thing with every major decision I make. I start by writing down a list of criteria."

"What do you mean by criteria?"

"I mean the things that are important to me in a job. For example, job security is really important to me."

"Bookkeepers definitely have job security."

"Yes, we do. Plus, I really enjoy organizing things. In marketing, I wasn't doing much organizing, so that interest wasn't being used. Finally, I wanted a predictable work schedule. Since I have a husband and two kids, I want to be home every evening to spend time with them."

"So let me get this straight. Your criteria were job security, organizational duties, and a predictable work schedule?"

Sandy smiled. "When you put it like that, I sound pretty boring. But yes, those were my criteria. That's why bookkeeping is a great fit for me. What's more secure, more organized, and more predictable than bookkeeping?"

Lisa thought for a moment and chose her words carefully. "I don't mean to offend you, Sandy, but those are some of the things I hate about bookkeeping."

Sandy smiled. "No offense taken. Bookkeeping isn't for everyone. It takes a passion for organizing things and an interest in routine. Judging from the mess on your desk and your scattered work schedule, it may not be for you."

Lisa felt a bit hurt. "Are you saying I'm not good at it?"

"No, you're really good at it. But you don't have to do something just because you're good at it. I'm saying you don't seem to like it."

"Well, I can't argue with that."

"Maybe it's time to figure out what you really want to do."

"I wouldn't even know where to start."

"It's a good thing we have another hour left on our drive. If you're willing, I want to try an experiment to see if we can find what's right for you."

Lisa grimaced. "I guess I don't have a choice. What else am I going to do for the next hour?"

Sandy asked Lisa to describe what she enjoyed most. "It could be a previous job that you loved, a hobby that you enjoy, or a class in school that you liked."

Lisa thought for a moment. "The things that come to mind are puzzles. I love putting together puzzles. When I was a kid, I would spend hours on puzzle games: crosswords, Sudoku, games like that. There's something about putting all the pieces together in a way that fits. I really enjoy that."

"OK. What's your favorite type of TV show?"

Lisa didn't see the connection, but she decided to play along. "It's probably detective shows. I love seeing how they track down clues and uncover the truth. I also like the way they keep asking people questions until they discover something interesting."

"Now, one more question. What are the most important things you're looking for in a job? They could be things like job security, friendly co-workers, a predictable work schedule, lots of travel, a specific geographic location, things like that."

"I've never really thought about it." Lisa paused. "Maybe having variety in what I do. That was my favorite part about working at my parents' diner. Every day was different, unlike what I'm doing now. Plus, I want to be putting together pieces of a puzzle, not just pulling the data and formatting it into reports."

"Good. I'm going to do a quick internet search of jobs that offer variety and involve solving puzzles. Give me a few minutes to find some examples."

Sandy tapped on her phone, occasionally murmuring things like, "No" and "Here's something interesting." Finally, she said, "I found a few options. Let's start with a police detective. You might need a degree in criminal justice and a few years of experience as a cop."

Lisa gave Sandy a sideways glance. "Next."

Sandy scrolled down on her phone. "Here's another one. An engineer. You'd need an engineering degree, which includes classes in physics, advanced math, and things like that. How does that sound?"

Lisa let out a sigh. "Next."

After a few more attempts, Sandy said "How about a market research analyst? They collect data, interpret it, and develop business recommendations. It says here that you would need to be a good problem solver and hungry for knowledge."

Lisa perked up. "You may be onto something. Tell me more."

Sandy found a few more job descriptions for market research analysts, and she read them to Lisa. After the third one, Lisa's voice was filled with excitement.

"That's it! That's what I'm looking for!"

Sandy grinned. "Great. Now let's start our tracker."

"Start our what? You get me all excited about a new job, and now you want me to work on that tracker. I really hate that tracker."

Sandy seemed confused. "Huh? Oh! I didn't mean our weekly sales tracker. I meant your Job Hunting Tracker."

"My what?"

"Your Job Hunting Tracker. It will keep track of all the jobs you want to apply for. As we search for jobs, we'll record all the details about each opportunity in one place."

Lisa signed. "Good. You had me worried there."

"Here's how it's gonna work. I'll search around on job sites while you keep driving. When I find a good market research job, I'll enter it onto your tracker."

"That sounds great. There's only one problem."

"What's that?"

"My parents' house. That's it up on the left. While I'd love to keep working on this, they're expecting us."

"That's fine. We'll have a two-hour drive back tomorrow. We'll work on it then. Now, it's time for you to get into little sister mode. Your big sister'll need your help with her wedding planning."

After a busy weekend with her family, Lisa couldn't wait to get back into her car with Sandy. As soon as she got behind the wheel, she turned to Sandy. "Now, about that tracker. Can we get started?"

Sandy smiled. "That's odd. I've never seen you so excited about working on a tracker." Sandy pulled her laptop out of a large tote bag. She opened it up and started typing on the keyboard.

"I'll just connect my laptop to my phone's hotspot, and we'll start surfing for jobs."

Lisa pulled her car onto the road and began driving back to the city. After a few minutes, Sandy said, "I found a good job site. Let's start by choosing some filters. First, let's talk location. How close do you want to stay to where you work now?"

"I really like the neighborhood where I live. Can we start with jobs that are an easy commute from midtown—maybe within ten miles?"

"Yep, I'm entering that as our first filter. I'll enter 'market research' as the type of job. Let's see what pops up. Hmm. That's strange. It says there are 1,594 jobs. That can't be right. Oh yeah, I forgot. On these sites, if you enter two words, it will give you any job that includes either word in the job description. Let me put quotes around those two words.

"OK, that's better: 269 jobs. Now let me try 'market research analyst' and see what comes up. Sixteen jobs. We can work with that."

"I'm amazed that there are sixteen jobs for market research analysts near where I live. That seems like a lot."

"It must be a popular field. I'll read you some job descriptions. You tell me which ones you want on your tracker. Here's one in uptown. It says that you'd be writing surveys and collecting data. You'd also be interpreting that data and making recommendations to people who do marketing."

"That sounds interesting. Do you think I'm qualified to do that?"

"Let me look at the requirements. It says you'd need an Associate's or Bachelor's degree and a strong knowledge of database software programs."

"Check and check. What else does it say?"

"You'd have to conduct research and convert your findings into understandable tables, graphs, and written reports."

"Sign me up. That sounds great."

"OK, that job goes onto our tracker." Sandy opened a blank spreadsheet and typed the necessary job details into the appropriate columns.

"I'm also gonna download this job description, so we can refer back to it later."

They spent the next hour discussing job descriptions and building Lisa's Job Hunting Tracker. They found twenty-one more jobs with titles that included Insights Coordinator, Research Assistant, and Data Analyst.

Lisa was starting to feel overwhelmed. "It seems like we have too many jobs on our list. Shouldn't we narrow it down a bit?"

"No, we need to cast a wide net. Now that we have a good list, we can prioritize the jobs. That'll make it more manageable. Let's go back through it and pick the ones that seem like the best fit for you."

For the remainder of the trip, Sandy read the details of each job to Lisa. Lisa had to decide how interested she was in each one. Sandy counted up the results.

"We have six top-tier choices, ten mid-tier, and five bottom-tier. We'll focus on the top-tier choices first."

"Great, what do we do next?"

"Next, we take a break. We're almost home. I'll email you the tracker, so you can look it over and make any changes you want. Then, let's get together later this week to start working on your resume."

"Sounds good to me. I'm really excited about this. Thanks for your help."

"My pleasure," Sandy said as they pulled up to the front of her house. Sandy said goodbye and got out of the car. As Lisa drove away, she realized that for the first time in years, she was excited about work. She finally had hope that things might turn around for her.

Review #1:
Build Your Strategy

As you've seen from our story, building a job-hunting strategy may seem intimidating at first. However, there are plenty of shortcuts.

You can start by browsing through some outstanding websites that are full of information about careers and employers. These sites include the Bureau of Labor Statistics site (www.bls.gov/ooh) and job sites like CareerBuilder, Job.com, Indeed, and Monster. Sites like these can help you figure out exactly what type of job you want so that you can more quickly develop your list of targeted companies.

Search for listings in your desired career field. As you find jobs that look interesting, enter them on your Job Hunting Tracker. See the Reference Materials in the back of the book for a sample tracker. Also, you'll want to remember to add any possibilities that you've learned about from friends, family members, or anywhere else.

Next, organize your list into tiers, with top-tier jobs being the ones you find most interesting. Before you apply for those jobs, you'll want to polish your resume, as shown in the next chapter.

It's very important that you DO NOT send out a standard resume to your top-tier employers. You should take the time to modify your resume for each of the employers that interest you most. If you send resumes to your lower-tier prospects, you can use a standardized resume, but your top-tier jobs deserve the extra attention that I'll describe next.

Now, start building your list of potential employers and prioritize them based on the criteria that are important to you. Again, refer to the Reference Materials in the back of the book for a template designed to help you build your job-hunting strategy.

2. Customize Your Resume

Creating a great resume is the next step in getting the job you want. Most employers require that you submit a resume with your initial application. The people who make employment decisions will use your resume to determine whether you make it to the next step of their screening process. That's why getting your resume right is so important.

The secret to writing a resume involves the employer's job description. In a job description, employers tell you exactly what they want to see. To move your resume to the top of their pile, you should use key words taken from their job description in your resume.

Finding the job descriptions should be easy. Typically, employers include them on the same websites where job openings are posted. If not, you can contact your target employers to see if they'll send you a job description directly.

Once you have a job description, start circling key words such as "analyze data, design brochures, and assist clients." Then, put as many of those key words as possible onto your resume. Most employers love seeing words from their job descriptions repeated back to them on resumes. This mimicking process shows that you understand the type of work that they need done and you have some experience doing it.

Obviously, you should only include experiences on your resume that are truthful. You should never lie on your resume. That could have severe consequences. Plus, it's just plain wrong. You should, however, include any experiences you have that closely match what employers have listed on their job descriptions.

More than ever, employers are using software programs called application tracking systems (ATS) to filter through resumes. Many employers only look at resumes after they have made it through the software's screening process. The use of the key words from the job description is your ticket for getting the ATS software to choose your resume. If the software program uses a job description for its search criteria, which is often the case, inserting key words from the job description into your resume will increase your odds of getting selected.

If you already have a draft of your resume, place it next to your targeted job descriptions. Check to see how well your bullet points match the duties listed. If a job description says that you'll be developing training programs, your resume should list any experience you have with developing training programs. If it states that the employer wants someone to process invoices, your resume should include any experience you have processing invoices.

Typically, people write their resumes based on the amount of time they've spent on the tasks in their previous jobs. Most employers don't care about time allocation. They care about the relevant experience you've gained. In their job descriptions, they tell you exactly what experiences are required for their respective companies. You just have to repeat those experiences back to them on your resume.

You should go through your work history and think about experiences you've had that most closely relate to the duties for the jobs you want. Write your experiences in brief phrases that match the job description language as closely as possible.

As a corporate recruiter, I love seeing resumes that include experience related to the job I'm hiring for. Plus, I appreciate a resume that looks like it's been customized. If you put forth the effort to customize your resume, you're the kind of person I want working at my company. Again, we don't care how much time you've spent on all the tasks you've ever done. We care about the experiences you've gained that are related to the duties on our job descriptions. Using this trick will make it easy for us to see your relevant experiences. It will also make it simple to select you for the next stage of the process, which is the job interview.

Use this trick for all the jobs on your top-tier list. It really doesn't take that long to customize a resume. Once you've built the first draft of your resume, plan on spending less than an hour to customize and proofread each version. When you think about how long you'll be working for a company, an hour is very little time to help your chances of getting that job.

Also, recruiters love to see numbers on resumes, so make sure you include as many measurable results as possible. If your actions resulted in a $50,000 increase in sales, include that on your resume. If you did something that saved your organization $5,000, include that. If you created a process that reduced the time to complete tasks by 20%, put that on your resume.

We also love to see awards, promotions, and leadership positions. You should include any relevant awards and contests you've won. For example, if you're going into engineering, record the fact that you've won first place in a science fair. Were you ever selected as employee of the month? Include that. It would be great to know if you were elected to be your class treasurer, especially if you're applying for an accounting job.

Finally, it's nice to see some unusual things listed in the Additional Information section of a resume. Throw in an unusual hobby. It will let the recruiter know that you might be more interesting than other candidates. I once agreed to interview someone just because they listed storm chasing as one of their interests. The rest of his resume wasn't impressive, but I really wanted to ask him about his hobby.

Don't leave out interests that show dedication. Examples include running marathons, completing Eagle Scout certification, and climbing mountains. If someone can complete those challenges, they'll be more likely to complete challenging work assignments.

Finally, keep your resume to one page. Resumes that are several pages typically include too much unrelated content or tend to be too repetitive.

The best resumes have four sections on a single page:

- **Contact Information**: This, of course, is your name, mailing address, email address, and phone number.
- **Education**: If you've gone to college, include your university, degree status, graduation date, and key activities, like student organizations and sports. If not, include that same information for your high school experience.
- **Experience**: List the two or three most relevant jobs for the career you want. Include a few short bullet points that describe the experiences you had in each job. Remember to include specific results that you achieved, promotions that you earned, and awards that you received.
- **Additional Information**: Include any volunteer positions, relevant certifications, interests, and key accomplishments outside of work. Make sure you include a few activities that might be intriguing to a potential employer.

Remember, don't be too wordy on your resume. Don't include things that are unrelated to the job, other than a few eye-catching interests. As a recruiter who often looks at dozens of resumes for each job opening, I always choose the ones that are short and to the point.

Let's see what the character in our story does to polish her resume.

Lisa and Sandy
Part 2

Lisa and Sandy agreed to meet for lunch later that week. They found a quiet conference room where they could have a private conversation while they ate. Sandy opened her brown paper lunch bag, took out a sandwich, and asked, "How's your Job Hunting Tracker coming?"

"Much better than my weekly sales tracker. I'm really enjoying the process of hunting down jobs that might be a good fit for me. I now have a list of seven jobs that I think are perfect, plus about twenty more that might be good options."

"That's great. Now, we'll start working on your resume."

"I'm way ahead of you. I've already finished my resume. I'm ready to start sending it out."

Sandy had a quizzical look on her face. "Do you mind if I take a look at it?"

"I don't mind at all. I emailed a copy to myself so I could forward it to employers." Lisa unlocked her phone and started tapping on her screen. "Here it is." Lisa handed her phone to Sandy.

Sandy looked at the screen for a moment as she scrolled down. "Hmm... How do I say this?"

Lisa looked confused. "What, you don't like it?"

Sandy looked uncomfortable. "Lisa, I'm going to be straight with you. This is bad...really bad. You didn't send this to anyone yet, did you?"

"Not yet. I'm planning to start sending it out tomorrow."

"Good. We caught it just in time. I'm gonna give you some tips for, well, polishing this a bit."

"Is that a nice way of saying that I have to start all over?"

"Not completely. There is some good information in here. There's also a lot that employers won't care about. It looks like it's about three pages long. I'd like you to get it down to a single page with just the really important stuff on it."

"I can't do that. I have way too many jobs to summarize them down to one page."

"You have done a lot, but most of it isn't stuff an employer will care about. I'll show you a trick for including just what they want to see. You'll need your laptop, so go get it and let's meet back here in five minutes."

Lisa went to her cubicle and grabbed her laptop and a notepad. When she got back to the conference room, Sandy told her, "Lisa, I don't want you to take any of this personally. When I started my job hunt, my resume looked a lot like yours. I included every work experience I could think of, whether it was relevant for the job I wanted or not. Then, I read a great book with tips for writing resumes. What I'm about to show you is from that book. It really helped me."

Lisa still looked hurt. "OK. I just don't see what's wrong with my resume. I put all of the jobs I've ever had and my duties for each one. Isn't that what a resume's supposed to be?"

"Actually, no. A resume should be the most relevant experiences you've had that relate to the job you want, not everything you've ever done. Let me show you what I mean. Please pull up the job description for one of your top-tier listings."

Lisa started tapping on her keyboard. "Here it is...my top choice is for a Market Research Analyst at a company called Premier Sporting Goods."

"Good. Now read off one of the job duties."

"OK. Gather data about consumers, competitors, and market conditions."

"Well, have you ever gathered data?"

"Of course. One of my duties here is to gather the sales data from all of our regions."

"Good. I want the first bullet point under your current job to start with 'gather data.' What's the next duty on the job description?"

"Prepare reports and present recommendations to management."

"Have you ever done that?"

"Not in my current job. I really don't make recommendations. I just enter data into our bookkeeping program and spreadsheets."

"Have you ever done anything that involved preparing reports?"

Lisa thought for a moment. "When I was in college, I was a teacher's assistant. I would summarize the research that the students did and prepare reports for my professor."

Sandy looked through Lisa's resume. "I don't see anything on here about you being a research assistant."

"I didn't get paid. I thought you were only supposed to include paid positions on your resume."

"False. You should include any relevant positions on your resume, whether they're paid or not. Being a teacher's assistant and preparing reports seems extremely relevant. Let's add it."

"Alright."

On her notepad, Lisa wrote research assistant. "What should I say about it?"

"Put down a bullet point that says 'prepared reports that summarized research conducted by students and made recommendations to professor.'"

Lisa paused. "It doesn't seem right to include the exact words from the job description. Shouldn't I change the words 'prepared reports' to something else? I don't want to plagiarize their job description."

Sandy smiled. "It's not plagiarism. It's making it easy for recruiters to see your experiences that line up with the job they're looking for. Plagiarism is when you take credit for something that someone else has written.

You're taking credit for something that you've done, not what someone else has written. Now, did any of your work lead to any publication?"

"Yes, the professor published four articles that included my recommendations."

"Great. At the end of that bullet point, put 'that were included in four published articles.' Now read me the full bullet point."

"Prepared reports that summarized research conducted by students and made recommendations to professor that were included in four published articles."

"It's a bit long, but let's leave it for now. We'll polish it later."

Lisa and Sandy spent the next half hour identifying experiences that related to the key duties from the job description. When they were done, they had included three jobs: Lisa's current bookkeeping job, her research assistant job, and her job as the assistant manager at her parents' restaurant.

Lisa looked at her original resume. "What about the other jobs I've had? When I was in college, I did everything from making deliveries to working as a cashier. Shouldn't those jobs be on my resume?"

"Are any of them related to the requirements in the job description?"

Lisa looked over the job description. "Not really."

"Then, you don't need to list them. You should only include your relevant experiences. There is one exception. You should include a few of your interests at the bottom of your resume."

"Even if they're not related to the job I want?"

"Yep. The purpose of the 'Interests' section is to give the employer extra information about who you are. Can you think of any hobbies or awards you've won that are interesting?"

Lisa thought for a moment. "I like running. I was the captain of my cross-country team in high school."

"That's good. It shows that you're willing to work hard and that you have some experience leading a team. Anything else?"

"I write blog articles in my spare time. Could that be relevant?"

"Absolutely. Let's put that down. It shows that you might be able to write interesting reports as a market researcher."

Sandy looked at the notes Lisa had written, gave her a few formatting tips, and asked to see an updated resume in a few days.

"When you have the next draft ready, I'll be your proofreader. We'll want to review it several times, because it's important there aren't any mistakes on your resume."

Over the next few days, Lisa and Sandy polished the first version of Lisa's resume. Then, Sandy instructed Lisa to submit it for the job opening at Premier Sporting Goods.

Next, they modified Lisa's resume to match the job descriptions for her other top-tier options. In the end, they submitted six different versions for all of her top job prospects.

"Now what?" Lisa asked.

"Now, we update your Job Hunting Tracker with the dates you submitted your resumes. It's also a good idea to submit resumes to your second-tier prospects. You don't have to spend as much time customizing your resume for them, since they're not as important to you."

"I already have six applications in the works. Isn't that enough?"

"It depends on how quickly you want things to move. If you're not in a hurry, having five or six applications in play at time is OK. If you want to speed things up, you can apply for more jobs than that. When I was looking for a job, I had over a dozen applications in at once. You just need to keep your tracker up to date so you can keep track of the jobs you've applied for."

"I think I want to stop at six for now. What do we do while we wait to hear back?"

"You'll need to start practicing for interviews. When an employer likes your resume, they'll want to interview you. I have a great book that'll help you prepare. I'll bring it to the office tomorrow, and I'll help you practice. We can start our practice sessions next week."

Sandy picked up her empty lunch bag, stood up, and started walking back towards her cubicle. "Between now and our next meeting, I want you to start reading the book. There's a chapter called, 'Opening Questions.' Make sure you finish that chapter so you'll be ready to start practicing." They agreed to meet for lunch twice a week to work on Lisa's interview skills.

Review #2:
Customize Your Resume

Now that Lisa has polished her resume, let's review why a good resume is so important.

Resumes are typically the first impression recruiters will have of you. You want to present yourself as a compelling and relevant choice for the positions they're trying to fill.

I've seen thousands of resumes over the years. Many of them were far too long. Often, job candidates included details about every job they ever had. That's completely unnecessary. Recruiters don't want to see your life history. They just want to see what you've done that's related to the role they're trying to fill.

Another common issue with resumes is a lack of relevant information. I love to see resumes that make it clear that the candidates understand the position they're applying for. Resumes accomplish this when they list experiences relevant to the open position without including too much unrelated information.

As a reminder, the secret to a great resume can be found in a job description. Employers are telling you exactly what they're looking for. They want to interview candidates who have experience related to their open positions. Write your resume to include primarily those relevant experiences.

Obviously, you should never lie about your experiences on your resume. You should always be truthful about everything. I've seen candidates include inaccurate or exaggerated information. When I've asked detailed questions or done fact-checking with previous employers, the truth invariably came out. If I find that a candidate has put anything misleading on their resume, I immediately remove that candidate from consideration. I also tell our Human Resources department to flag that candidate to ensure we don't hire them in the future.

If a recruiter suspects that you've been untruthful about information on your resume or during an interview, the consequences could be severe. The employer will likely immediately remove you from consideration for their job. If, after they hire you, they find out you had inaccurate information on your resume, they will still have grounds to fire you immediately.

If you feel like you have no relevant experiences for the job you want, that's OK. Now is the time to get those experiences. You can almost always find a part-time job, a hobby, or a volunteer position to build your credentials. Again, start with the job description you consider to be your top priority position, and then look for experiences that will help you build the necessary skills to get that job.

One of the best things you can do for your career is to study job descriptions for the type of career you want. Then, find jobs or projects that give you experiences related to those job descriptions.

If you need ideas for finding relevant experiences, talk to your friends, your family members, or a career coach. Then, go get that experience and put it on your resume.

Refer to the Reference Material section of this book for templates and examples to help you build your winning resume.

3. Practice for Opening Questions

Now you should start preparing for interviews. Since most recruiters use a similar format for their interviews, we'll focus on the three most common types of questions: opening questions, fit questions, and case questions.

Let's start with opening questions. The most common question in any job interview is: "Can you tell me about yourself?" This is the recruiter's way of seeing if you can communicate relevant information about yourself. Your response will set the tone for the rest of the interview. If you nail it, you'll start with a strong first impression. The recruiter will be rooting for you throughout the rest of the interview. If you bomb it, the recruiter may rule you out before you get to the next question.

My favorite way to answer this question to use a technique called the P-E-N framework. This framework can be extremely powerful for organizing your answers in clear, compelling ways. The P-E-N framework can be used to answer a variety of opening questions, including the following:

- Can you tell me about yourself?
- Will you walk me through your resume?
- Can you tell me why you're interested in this job?
- Why should I hire you?

With strong answers to these questions, you'll distinguish yourself from other candidates who want the same jobs you want. You should keep practicing and refining your answers to these questions until you have responses that will absolutely dazzle recruiters.

First impressions are incredibly powerful, so developing winning answers to opening questions should be the most important part of your interview preparation. Your answers should be fairly brief, lasting less than two minutes. Include highlights from your work experience, but don't go into detail about any specific job. You want to give an overview of your background, not an in-depth story about any particular experience.

Use the P-E-N framework for these questions. P-E-N stands for passion, experience, and next. Your well-practiced answer, using this framework, will show that you're a better choice than other candidates who might give unstructured answers or irrelevant details about themselves.

P is for PASSION:

Start by telling the recruiter what you're passionate about. Make sure you choose a passion that's related to the job you want. Recruiters are looking for people who will enjoy their work. Let them know how you feel.

For example, someone in the accounting field might say, "I'm an organizer. I really enjoy organizing things into neat, orderly groups." Someone applying for a consulting job might say, "I love strategy. I enjoy defining clear objectives and identifying the best options to meet those objectives."

Now, go back to the job descriptions for your targeted companies and figure out what passions you have that relate to the duties for those jobs.

E is for EXPERIENCE:

Summarize experiences that are relevant for the job you want. You should do this briefly. This will give the interviewer context for the rest of the interview.

Our aspiring accountant might say, "I'm the treasurer for my school's accounting club. In that role, I've put in place a new bookkeeping system that makes it easier for us to see where we're spending our money." Our consultant could say, "My interest in strategy helped me to win my high school's chess competition. Chess is all about knowing which options are best to accomplish your objective. Identifying those options and prioritizing them is something I'm especially good at."

Look over your resume and think about the work experiences that are most relevant for the jobs you want. Summarize those experiences into a few sentences.

N is for NEXT:

Tell the interviewer the type of experience you'd like next. Your answer should be directly related to the role they're trying to fill. Below are examples for the N section of the P-E-N framework.

Our accountant might say, "Next, I'm looking for a job where I can apply my passion for organizing things. I'd like to work for your accounting firm, where I can build my skills in bookkeeping, auditing, and tax accounting."

Our aspiring consultant could end with, "Next, I want to find a job that will help me accomplish my goal of becoming a more effective business consultant. I've researched my options, and I believe your company is the best fit for my skills and interests. Hopefully, you'll see that I'm a great choice for what you're looking for."

Let's see how Lisa goes about practicing for opening questions.

Lisa and Sandy
Part 3

The next day, Sandy gave Lisa the interview book she had promised. That night, Lisa started reading it. The book was filled with useful tips about answering interview questions, along with frameworks Lisa could use to organize her answers.

When she met with Sandy for their next session, she was ready to start practicing. Sandy was sitting in the conference room when Lisa arrived. "Hey Lisa, grab a seat. Did you get a chance to look at the book?"

Lisa sat down and set her resume on the table in front of her. "Yep. It was really good. I spent some time practicing my answers to the opening questions. I'm ready to work on those if you are."

"I'm ready. So Lisa, can you tell me about yourself?"

Lisa smiled. "I've always been passionate about puzzles. Ever since I was a kid, I've liked all kinds of puzzle games like crosswords, Sudoku, and other games like that.

"That's part of what led me to get my associate's degree in finance. I like using data to see what story it can tell me. It's like putting the pieces of a puzzle together.

"While working as a research assistant in college, I found that if I could get all the pieces of information to fit just right, it would lead me to clear conclusions. Then, I could make informed recommendations.

"After I graduated, I joined Beacon Medical Services as a bookkeeper. My favorite part of my job is collecting data, interpreting it, and developing recommendations for the people who make key business decisions. It reminds me of putting all of the pieces of a puzzle together in such a way that everything fits.

"Now, I'm looking for a job where I can grow my skills. I'd like even more challenging puzzles to solve. That's why I'm interested in being a research analyst for your company."

Sandy paused. "That was a good start. I like the way you explained your passion. Your experiences were clear. You did a good job on relating what you want to do next. I'd like you to work on the experience section a bit more.

Let's talk about other examples of work you've done that are related to what a research analyst does."

They spent the rest of the hour polishing Lisa's response to the question: "Can you tell me about yourself?"

At their next meeting, Sandy started by asking Lisa why she was interested in the research analyst job.

Lisa asked, "Should I assume that I've already told the recruiter about myself?"

"No, assume that this is the first question in the interview."

"OK, I'll use the same P-E-N framework. Here it goes. I'm interested in this job because of my passion for solving puzzles. I've always loved tracking down information and putting it together in a way that tells an interesting story, much like putting the pieces of a puzzle together to see the whole picture.

"As you can see from my resume, I studied finance at Northern College. While I was there, I learned to use data to figure out what was really happening with a business. I was also a staff reporter for my school's newspaper. My specialty was investigative reporting. I tracked down all of the information needed to tell a clear story. I really enjoyed that.

"I'm currently working as a bookkeeper at Beacon Medical Services. I'm getting great experience, using various data sources and analyzing information. While I enjoy the analytics, the work I do is fairly routine. I really enjoy learning. My current job doesn't involve the types of projects that encourage me to build new skills.

"Now, I'm looking for a job where I can have more variety in the work I do. I want to learn more effective ways to conduct research. My understanding is that your research analyst role would give me an opportunity to collect data, interpret it, and develop business recommendations for a wide variety of projects. Since I love solving puzzles, that's exactly the kind of role I'm looking for."

Sandy smiled. "That was really good. I think you're almost ready to move on to the next type of question. Let's spend another week or two practicing your interview skills. If an employer likes your resume, they may want you to interview right away, and I want to make sure you're ready."

"What if my favorite job prospects all get filled?"

"There will always be more jobs to apply for."

"But I feel prepared. I want to get started now."

Sandy paused. "If you're prepared, tell me about a time you've led a complex project."

"Well. Um. I ... I ... That's not fair. I wasn't ready for that question."

"No, you weren't. You're not ready for a lot of questions. Next, we're going to practice your answers to fit questions. Then we'll work on case questions."

"Ugh. How long will that take?"

"If you do your homework, you can get there in two or three weeks. That might seem like a long time, but it's nothing compared to how long you've been in a job you hate."

"Good point. What's my homework?"

"There's a chapter in the book I gave you about fit questions. Read it and start preparing your S-T-A-R stories."

"My what stories?"

"You'll see. Just read the book."

They agreed to meet a few days later. Lisa and Sandy left the conference room and went back to work. That night, Lisa went home and started reading the next chapter in her book.

Review #3:
Practice for Opening Questions

As you can see from our story, it's much easier to answer interview questions when you have a good framework. For opening questions, use the P-E-N framework so that recruiters can find out what you're passionate about, what relevant experience you have, and what you want to do next.

When recruiters ask you to tell them about yourself, you may think they want to hear about your personal life. They really don't. They want to hear why you'll be a good choice for the job they have to offer. Limit your answers to information that directly relates to the job, unless they say otherwise.

Now that you know how to approach opening questions, practice your answers using the P-E-N framework. You'll be ready to move onto the next type of questions before you know it.

See the Reference Materials section in the back of this book for sample opening questions as well as worksheets to use for your answers.

4. Practice for Fit Questions

The second type of question in the interview process is called a fit question. A recruiter may ask these questions to determine whether you'll be a good fit for their organization. One common example is: "What's your greatest strength?" Your answers will tell recruiters a lot about your personality and how well you might fit in with their company culture.

Here are additional examples of fit questions that you might hear during an interview:

- What do you think is your biggest weakness?
- Can you tell me about a time when you've demonstrated analytical skills?
- Can you tell me about your leadership style?
- How would you handle a situation if you had to deal with a difficult person on a project?
- Have you ever developed a creative solution to a challenging problem?

My favorite way to answer fit questions is using the S-T-A-R framework. When used effectively, this framework will impress recruiters with your communication skills and your ability to get results. The S-T-A-R stands for Situation, Task, Actions, and Result. It's the easiest way to structure clear, compelling responses. Here's how it works:

S is for SITUATION:

Start with one sentence that describes a situation. This could be as simple as stating where you were working and giving your job title.

T is for TASK:

In one sentence, tell the interviewer what your assignment was. This could be a task assigned to you by an employer, a teacher, or a peer.

A is for ACTIONS:

In a few sentences, explain the actions you took to complete your task. Don't talk about what a group of people did. Recruiters want to hear about the actions you, specifically, took to make things happen.

R is for RESULT:

Tell the recruiter about the results that transpired from your efforts. If possible, quantify those results or explain how you delivered something above and beyond what the task called for.

Here's an example that shows how a graphic artist might use the S-T-A-R framework to answer the fit question: "Can you tell me about a time when you solved a problem with a creative approach?"

Situation: "I was a freelance designer working on a project for a local smoothie shop."

Task: "My client wanted me to redesign their online menu."

Actions: "I spent an afternoon at the smoothie shop, where I asked customers what they liked most about the place. They told me they liked the cheerful atmosphere and fresh fruits that were used in the smoothies. Since I knew what customers liked most, I designed the new online menu with bright, cheerful colors. I included images of fresh fruits."

Result: "Since the smoothie shop switched from their text-based online menu to my design with the bright colors and images of fresh fruits, their online orders have doubled."

Here's another example that shows how a salesperson might use the S-T-A-R approach to answer the fit question: "Can you tell me about a time when you used your persuasion skills?"

Situation: "I was working at the Eastern University bookstore as a sales representative."

Task: "My manager asked me to persuade the business school professors to recommend our store to their students."

Actions: "I hosted a free lunch for the professors, and I asked them questions during that event. They told me they were frustrated because their students might remember to buy textbooks, but they'd often forget to buy workbooks. I told the professors that my bookstore would bundle all the books for each class together so students would automatically get every book they needed, including the workbooks they might have forgotten otherwise. Then, I asked the professors to recommend my bookstore to their students."

Result: "The next semester, our sales of business books went up 30%. When we asked business students why they bought their books from our store, many of them said their professors recommended our store to them."

For fit-type questions, you should have five or six stories prepared. With the right stories, you can cover a broad range of questions. For example, you should have stories that will flex to address the following topics:

- Leadership, which includes building a team and getting results
- Creativity, including finding innovative solutions to challenging problems
- Collaboration, which could involve building relationships and demonstrating interpersonal skills
- Persistence, which means working through difficult situations

Once you prepare a few different S-T-A-R stories, you should practice adapting each story to answer a variety of fit questions.

Let's see how Lisa prepares for fit questions.

Lisa and Sandy
Part 4

Lisa arrived at her next meeting a few minutes early. She was excited to get started, but also a bit nervous. The more she learned about interviewing, the more she started to feel overwhelmed.

Sandy walked into the conference room holding her lunch bag and a cup of coffee. "Hey, Lisa. Are you ready for some fit questions?"

"I think so. I read the book. I have four or five S-T-A-R stories ready to go. Will that be enough for today?"

"Absolutely. If the stories are good, that might be all you'll need for every interview you have. Let's start with this one: Can you tell me your greatest strength?"

"OK. I'd have to say my greatest strength is my ability to track down information that can be used to make important decisions. When I was a reporter for my college newspaper, my assignment was to do a story on a new renovation that our school was planning for our computer lab.

"First, I interviewed the planning committee members. I learned that they had project management skills, but they didn't have any construction experience.

"Next, I found people who worked on planning committees for similar projects at other colleges. I interviewed them. I discovered some significant challenges they faced and how they addressed those challenges.

"Finally, I wrote an article from the perspective of how to avoid issues that often come up during big renovation projects. I shared that article with our school's planning committee before I published it. At my suggestion, they changed their plans to account for some of the issues that might have arisen as the renovation project progressed.

"As a result, our school saved an estimated $100,000 in construction costs. Also, the renovation timeline was cut by almost two months. As a bonus, the head of the planning committee recognized me as the student who made the biggest contribution to the project. That's just one example of how I've used my abilities to track down useful information and made an impact on important decisions."

Sandy nodded her head. "That was a great S-T-A-R story. Your situation and task were clear. Your actions were compelling. Your results were impressive. Well done. I can see how you could use that story for all kinds of questions, like how you demonstrated persistence, how you collaborated with others, and how you've had a big impact on an important project. Now, for a harder question: What's your biggest weakness?"

"Ugh. I hate that one. According to the book you gave me, I'm supposed to pick a weakness that's not related to the job I want. So here it goes. I'd say my biggest weakness is that I don't seek out the spotlight. I much prefer working behind the scenes, which has been an issue for me in the past. For example, when I was working on a sales tracker in my current job, I noticed that our sales for a particular product were declining in one of our regions. When something like that happens, my task is to call it out to management.

"I spent some time researching the issue, and I learned that a competitor was dropping their prices in that region. Then I prepared a report with a recommendation for how to address that competitive threat. Next, I emailed the report to my manager.

"I didn't realize how busy my manager was at the time. She didn't see the email. After a few weeks, I mentioned the issue to her. She didn't know what I was talking about. We lost a few weeks of response time, which wasn't a big issue, but I wish I had been more outspoken in the way I handled it.

"As a result of the experience, I've learned to seek out key decision makers in our company when I see a significant issue or opportunity. I know I can be effective working behind the scenes, but I also know that I can be more effective if I provide important information to the people who can use it."

Sandy nodded. "That was good. It's a really tough question. I like the way you ended with a result that shows what you learned and how you'll handle situations like that in the future.

"As an added bonus, I like the way your weakness demonstrates that you're willing to give your manager information that will make them look good, without trying to take all the credit yourself. That's the kind of weakness that some managers like. The more you can do to make them look good, the better."

Lisa and Sandy spent the rest of their lunch time together reviewing other S-T-A-R stories. After another week of practice, Lisa had six stories that demonstrated a wide variety of skills. She was feeling encouraged, right up until Sandy told her that the most difficult type of question was next: the case question.

Review #4:
Practice for Fit Questions

As you can see from our story, fit questions can be challenging. With these types of questions, recruiters appreciate real-life stories. By telling stories about actions you've taken and results you've gotten, you'll be demonstrating that you have and the experience needed to get things done.

One of my favorite sayings is "facts tell; stories sell." It means that people often don't make decisions based on facts. You can tell a recruiter your grade point average, how many months of work experience you have, and how many classes you've taken in specific subjects. Those are all facts, but they aren't very interesting.

Recruiters are more impressed by stories you tell about your experiences, especially if you include specific results you've gotten. That's why the S-T-A-R framework is so effective. It helps you to frame up stories that have a beginning, middle, and an end. In those stories, you are the hero. When you tell recruiters relevant stories about yourself, they'll remember you as the person who can do the types of things they want done.

For reference, here's an example of how *not* to answer a fit question such as: "Can you tell me about a time when you demonstrated leadership?"

"I've always been a great basketball player. In high school, I led my team in points per game and rebounds.

"I also once led a group of fellow Boy Scouts on a hike. We went to a beautiful national park. I was the fastest hiker in the group. I was so fast that the other kids had difficulty keeping up with me.

"Another time, I led my school's debate team with the highest number of wins in our competitions. I'm very competitive, so I worked hard at beating my team members. If you hire me, I'll bring that competitive spirit into your environment. I'll find a way to beat my co-workers at any goal you set for me."

First, this candidate gave too many examples. Each one was too brief to make a compelling point. A good answer to this question would focus on one story that included impressive results.

Also, this candidate doesn't seem to understand leadership. Rather than talking about being better than his teammates, he should have focused on how he built a team that successfully accomplished a goal together. Had he done so, the recruiter would see him as someone who could lead by motivating other people, not drive his co-workers crazy with his overly competitive nature.

Now, take a few minutes to go to the Reference Materials section in the back of this book and fill in the Fit Questions worksheets. Ideally, you should have five or six S-T-A-R stories you can use for a variety of questions.

5. Practice for Case Questions

The third type of question in interviews is called a case question. With case questions, recruiters ask you to explain how you'd handle specific job situations. They'll be testing your knowledge and your ability to exercise good judgment in a work situation.

Since most case questions are specific to particular career fields, you should find a list of case questions for the type of job you want. In this chapter, I'll explain how to answer case questions for certain career fields, including business, healthcare, engineering, and education. If you're in a different field, you may want to get advice for answering industry-specific case questions from online articles, videos, or books that specialize in your specific career field.

Here are few common case questions:

- Business: "If your company's sales were declining, what would you do?"
- Healthcare: "If a patient fainted in front of you, how would you respond?"

- Engineering: "If I asked you to design a new highway intersection, how would you approach that?"
- Education: "If a child was being disruptive in your class, what would you do?"

For case questions, recruiters might ask you to explain how you'd approach specific situations related to the job you want. They might ask you to explain how you'd address hypothetical situations, such as opportunities that arise in a business or emergencies that happen in a healthcare environment. They might also ask you to formulate a recommendation, assess a sample of someone's work, or make a persuasive argument.

Here are a few more examples of case questions you might hear in interviews:

- Marketing: "What would you do if you needed to launch a new product?"
- Healthcare: "How would you diagnose a patient who complained of chest pains?"
- Engineering: "If I asked you to design a bridge that needed to last 1,000 years, how would do that?"

- Computer Science: "What questions would you ask if you needed to upgrade a computer network?"
- Education: "If you had to explain algebra to a student, where would you start?"

Recruiters sometimes ask particularly challenging case questions to test how well you think on your feet or to see how you react in stressful situations. If you need a moment to gather your thoughts, you can start a response by asking a few clarifying questions. This will show that you assess a situation before jumping to a conclusion. It will also buy you some additional time to think of a good response.

You should also state your assumptions or your criteria for the answer you'll give. For example, if you're asked what your favorite medication is, you could start by saying that your answer would be based on criteria such as effectiveness in the treatment of a particular medical condition and the absence of adverse side effects. This approach works well because it shows the recruiter that you can formulate recommendations based on relevant criteria.

Let's see how Lisa goes about practicing for case questions.

Lisa and Sandy
Part 5

Lisa and Sandy started working on the last type of interview questions: case questions. At their next meeting, Lisa felt frustrated. "Sandy, I'm having trouble getting started with case questions. Since I've never worked in a research job, I'm not sure what kinds of case questions they might ask."

Sandy thought for a moment. "If only we had someone who was good at conducting research. They could find appropriate case questions for research jobs."

Lisa frowned. "OK, I get the hint. I can do the research, but can you help me?"

"Absolutely. Let's get our laptops and see what we can find."

Lisa and Sandy went back to their respective desks, grabbed their computers, and returned to the conference room. They each started searching for case questions related to the jobs Lisa wanted.

Lisa looked up from her laptop. "I found a site with sample questions for marketing, insights, and research positions. It also has some useful frameworks for interview answers."

"Great. What does it say?"

"One of the most common questions is: 'Can you tell me how you would investigate a situation in which your company's products weren't meeting your sales expectations?' There are suggestions for using the What, Who, Where, When, and Why framework to answer that question. That's funny. It's the same framework I learned when I was working at the college newspaper."

"It's actually not surprising. That seems like a framework that can be used for all kinds of jobs. Let's see it in action. Lisa, tell me what you'd do if your company's products weren't selling well."

"OK. I'd start with the 'What.' What is the specific problem to solve? You've already given me that, so I'll move on to the 'Who.' I'd find out who the target audience is. Then, I'd make sure that audience makes sense for the product we're trying to sell. Next, I'd go to the 'Where.' I'd want to know where we're selling our products. I'd see if we have the products in the places where potential customers could find them when they're making purchasing decisions. That leads me to the 'When'. I'd want to find out when our customers are most interested in products like mine. Finally, I'd end with the 'Why'. I'd put all the information together and determine why customers aren't buying the products as much as I'd like them to.

"Using this framework, I'd be able to find out if our products are being targeted to the wrong people, if we're distributing the products in the wrong places, if we're trying to sell them to customers when they're not interested, or if there could be another reason why they are not buying them."

Sandy wrote down a few notes on her notepad. "That was good. We can work on it a little more, but it's a nice start."

Lisa and Sandy spent another week practicing for case questions.

Review #5:
Practice for Case Questions

With case questions, recruiters want to see if you can think through challenging problems or address situations that might come up within the jobs they are trying to fill. Since those situations are specific to particular types of jobs, you should practice your case answers with people who are knowledgeable in your career field.

Often, the best place to get information about case questions in your field of interest is online. A simple Internet search may result in a list of case questions and recommended frameworks for your answers. If you're in a popular career field, you might also find books with tips for answering your case questions.

Another place to look is among people who are already doing the type of job you want to get. Most of them have gone through interviews like the ones you're preparing for, so they can give you advice. Since they are already doing the type of work that you'll be asked about, they can tell you how they approach that work.

As you can see from our story, case questions are much easier to answer when you have a framework in mind. For journalism and research jobs, you can use the

What, Who, Where, When, and Why framework. A common framework for marketing jobs is the 4-P's framework: Product, Placement, Pricing, and Promotion. Each career field has its own frameworks, so you need to do some research to see which frameworks might work best in your area of interest.

Take a few minutes now to think about how you'd answer case questions for your line of work. See if you can find frameworks that are common in your career field. Then, go to the Reference Materials section in the back of this book and practice the answers provided there.

Here are some dos and don'ts to remember when you're practicing your interview answers:

Dos:

- Limit most of your answers to about a minute or less. Each answer should be long enough to get the interviewer interested in you, but not so long that you're monopolizing the conversation.
- As you talk about your experiences, mention your biggest accomplishments, any promotions you've received, and any major awards you've won.

- Have five or six S-T-A-R stories ready to go. That way, you can answer a variety of fit questions.
- Limit your S (Situation), T (Task), and R (Result) to one or two sentences each. The recruiter wants to see that you can communicate succinctly, so spend your time on your actions, not the other aspects of your story.
- Be specific about your actions. Tell the recruiter exactly what you personally did.
- Make sure your results are clear and compelling. Always end your story with positive results. Recruiters are looking for problem solvers, so compelling results are a must. If you didn't get a positive result, use a different story.
- For case questions, use a framework that's relevant for your field of study. You can find those frameworks online or by talking with someone in that career field.
- If you don't have an immediate answer to the question, ask a few clarifying questions. That will demonstrate you can seek to understand a situation, rather than jumping straight to an answer without understanding the context.

Asking a few clarifying questions will also buy you time to think of your answer.

Don'ts:

- Don't include too much personal information in your answers, such as details about your family, friends, or hobbies that are unrelated to the job you want. Recruiters want to know why you would make a good employee. They really don't want to know about the personal details of your life.

- Don't be negative about anything. No matter how bad your previous jobs or bosses were, don't ever say anything negative about them during an interview. Recruiters want to hire positive people, so show them how positive you can be.

- Don't go into too much detail on any specific topic. The recruiters want to see that you can summarize information without getting caught up in details. Just give them high-level answers, and if you have the opportunity, go into the details later in the interview.

- Don't give a short, one-sentence answer. If you rush through your response, you could be seen as impulsive or lacking a depth of knowledge. You want to show recruiters that you can logically formulate a thoughtful answer.

- Don't say "we." Instead, say "I." Recruiters don't want to hear what a group of people did. They want to hear about what *you* did. When you say "we," your role is not clear in the story. Train yourself to always say "I" in your stories.
- Don't act like your answer is the only correct one. You might come off as arrogant or rigid if you act like your answer is the only option.

Now that you've practiced your interview skills, it's time to start applying for jobs and going to interviews.

6. NAIL YOUR INTERVIEWS

6. Nail Your Interviews

Your next objective should be to get interviews for your top-tier job prospects. This involves submitting your resumes in the way each recruiter prefers. If the job is posted on an online job site, submit your resume or an online application by following the site's instructions.

Make sure you customize each resume to match the job description for each of your top tier prospects. Since many sites require a cover letter, you'll also want to customize your cover letters. You should proofread every application, resume, and cover letter before you submit. I've seen candidates include the wrong company's name in a cover letter or submit resumes with basic spelling mistakes. Errors like that will make it easy for recruiters to rule you out before you even get a chance to interview.

You should send out resumes for six to ten jobs at a time. You may not hear back from many of the recruiters, so you'll want to have multiple resumes out at any given time. Make sure you update your Job Hunting Tracker with the dates you submitted your resumes, as well as dates and names for every interaction you have with each potential employer. Also, you should have an organized filing system detailing which resume you submitted for which job. That way, when it's time to interview, you'll take the correct resume to each interview.

Lisa and Sandy
Part 6

After Lisa submitted her resume to her top-tier companies, she waited over two weeks without hearing back from any of the employers.

Finally, she received an email from a regional restaurant chain.

Dear Ms. Brimmer,
We regret to inform you that we will not be asking you
to interview for the position for which you applied.

Lisa was crushed. How could this happen? She knew she had built an amazing resume for that company. It was a perfect match for their job description.

The next day, Lisa stopped at Sandy's desk.

"Sandy, I just got my first rejection. It's from that restaurant chain. It seemed like such a good fit."

"You've only gotten one rejection letter? In my first two weeks, I must have gotten a half a dozen."

"What? I thought you got a good job right away."

"I don't think anyone gets a good job right away. Finding a job takes time. You have to get used to rejection. It's part of the process."

"It may be part of the process, but I hate it. I hope I don't get any more."

"Oh, you will. I probably got four or five rejections for every offer to interview. I think I applied for about thirty jobs before I got my first offer."

"Thirty jobs! There's no way I could apply for thirty jobs. It took forever to apply to the half dozen I've done so far."

"Lisa, how important is it to you that you get a good job?"

"It's probably the most important thing I'm doing right now. I absolutely have to get out of the job I'm in now. If I have to keep doing these financial reports every day, it'll drive me crazy."

"OK. You need to put on your big girl pants, keep applying for jobs, and accept that rejection is part of the process."

Lisa went home that night and submitted four more applications. She also started calling friends and asking if any of them knew about companies that were hiring.

A week later, she received a call from a company. "Hi, Lisa. This is Barbara Gaines at Premier Sporting Goods. I'd like you to come to our office for an interview."

Lisa was overwhelmed with relief. She scheduled an interview with Barbara for the following Monday.

***

Once you schedule a job interview with a company, it's time to start cramming. You should start researching everything you can find about that company. Go online and review their website. See if you can find any articles about the company. If they sell products, try them out. If they own stores, go tour their stores. If you know people who work at the company, ask them to tell you about the environment. You'll want to be as familiar with them as possible.

Use that information to prepare for interview questions like: "Why do you want to work for our company?" and "What questions do you have for me?" Recruiters prefer to hire people who specifically want to work for their company. Figure out what it is about their organization that makes you want to work for them.

You should isolate specific things about their products or services that appeal to you. Maybe you used their products when you were growing up. Perhaps you like the way their services bring happiness to customers. Find something about them that you truly admire.

Let's see how Lisa approaches this research phase of the process.

Lisa and Sandy
Part 7

Lisa pulled up the Premier Sporting Goods website on her phone. She read the Company History section and learned that it was a family-owned business. Most of the executives were members of the Baxter family. She read through the bios for them.

Then, she went to online shopping sites and researched their products. It looked like they sold mainly baseball and golf equipment. The ratings for their products were generally favorable.

Next, Lisa started texting her friends, asking if any of them knew someone at Premier. One of her classmates from high school responded. He said that his cousin worked at the company and could put a good word in for her. Lisa then called that cousin and asked him about the company culture, business priorities, and working styles.

Lisa started thinking of reasons she would want to work for Premier. She thought about the benefits of working in a family-owned business. She considered her passion for sports. In high school, she had played golf. She seemed to remember having a set of Premier golf clubs. Maybe she could mention that during her interview.

Lisa called her mom and told her about the upcoming interview. "Mom, can you see if you can find my old golf clubs? I think they're in the garage."

Lisa could hear shuffling noises coming through the phone. Then, her mom said, "Yep, found 'em."

"Great. Can you read the brand name on the golf clubs?"

"It says Premier."

Lisa was excited. She thanked her mom, said goodbye, and hung up the phone.

Lisa now had a personal connection to the company that she could use in the interview. She spent the rest of the weekend practicing her interview answers and talking with friends who could give her advice.

On Sunday evening, she ironed her favorite blouse, laid out her interview suit, and picked out shoes that matched her outfit. She also chose a handbag that was big enough to hold a folder, a bottle of water, and a few snacks. She went to bed early that night. While it took her a while to get to sleep, she eventually got a good night of rest.

The next morning, she woke up early and ate a big breakfast. She packed a small bag of nuts and a bottle of water into her handbag. She also put ten copies of her resume into a nice folder and slid the folder into her handbag.

She checked the weather. There was no chance of rain. Good. She wouldn't need an umbrella. Then, she checked traffic. It was heavy that day, so she would need to leave her apartment early.

Lisa's interview was at 9:00 a.m. She left her apartment in time to get to the Premier office thirty minutes before the interview. As she hit unusually heavy traffic, Lisa started to panic. *What if she missed the interview?* As her car inched along, Lisa checked the navigation app on her phone. It said she'd get to her destination ten minutes before her interview started. She relaxed a bit. Ten minutes was cutting it close, but it was enough time to check in and calm down a bit after a rough commute.

When Lisa arrived, she parked in the visitors parking area. She put her cell phone into silent mode, walked into the front lobby, and checked in with the receptionist. She asked if she could use the restroom before the receptionist notified Barbara Gaines that she had arrived. The receptionist smiled and pointed in the direction of the ladies' room. Lisa went inside and checked herself out in mirror. She straightened her clothes, made sure her hair was neat, and checked to see that no lipstick was smudged on her teeth. She returned to the reception desk and politely requested that the receptionist notify Barbara that she had arrived.

A few minutes later, a well-dressed middle-aged woman entered the lobby. She walked up to Lisa and shook her hand.

"You must be Lisa. I'm Barbara. Thanks for coming a few minutes early. You'll be interviewing with me first. Then, you'll interview with Mr. Baxter."

"Which Mr. Baxter? I understand there are at least three Mr. Baxters here."

Barbara stopped walking and gave Lisa a smile. "Someone's done her homework. I'm impressed. There are three Mr. Baxter's, but there's only one we call Mr. Baxter."

"Is that the CEO, Ed Baxter?"

"Again, impressive. But, that's not him. He prefers to be called Ed. Our CFO, Francis Baxter, prefers to be called Mr. Baxter."

Lisa made a mental note that she might want to be more formal during her interview with that Mr. Baxter.

Barbara walked Lisa to a small conference room where they started their interview.

***

Preparing for an interview is like preparing for a big test. You should be doing your homework for weeks ahead of time. Cram in as much research as you can in the final days before to your big interview. In our story, Lisa did a great job researching the company and preparing answers that were specific to the company. You'll see how that pays off for her during the interview.

The night before your interview, try to get a good night of rest. Many people get restless before interviews, so sleep may be difficult. Try to go to bed early, even if you're not able to sleep right away. That way, you'll at least be resting.

Set an alarm to wake up early on the interview day. Eat a big breakfast and pack a snack in case you get hungry later. You should also pack a bottle of water so you can stay hydrated throughout the interview process. While some companies may only have hour-long interviews, others may want you to interview for as much as a full day.

Arrive at least thirty minutes early. If traffic is light, you can wait in your car, a nearby coffee shop, or a reception area until about fifteen minutes before your scheduled interview time. If traffic is heavy, you'll have extra time built in so you won't arrive late.

If you don't build in this extra commute time, you risk arriving late, which is one of the worst things you can do. Many recruiters will automatically eliminate candidates who show up for interviews late. Don't risk it.

When you arrive at the building where you'll be interviewing, find a restroom and use it. You definitely want to make sure you don't need to use a restroom if you end up in back-to-back interviews for a few hours. Also, you should make one final check in the restroom mirror to ensure that you look sharp. Check to see that your clothes are neat, your hair looks good, and you don't have anything stuck in your teeth.

Check in with the receptionist about ten minutes before your scheduled interview time. Turn your cell phone to silent mode and wait patiently. This is a good time to look over your resume and think about your interview responses.

When you meet your interviewer, greet them with a friendly smile and a firm handshake. As a recruiter, I always enjoy seeing friendly, cheerful job candidates.

Now, let's see how Lisa's interview process goes.

Lisa and Sandy
Part 8

After sitting, Barbara started the conversation.

"I'll tell you about our interview process. Then, we'll get into the interview. I'm the hiring manager. I'm looking for someone to fill our research analyst position. I'll ask you some questions to see if you might be a good fit for the job. Then, you'll interview with Mr. Baxter. We like having one of our executives interview each candidate.

"To start, can you walk me through your resume?"

Lisa noticed that Barbara didn't have a copy of her resume, so she took out her folder. She pulled out two copies of her resume, handed one to Barbara, and put the other one in front of herself.

Lisa silently reminded herself to follow her P-E-N framework: Passion, Experience, Next.

"You'll notice a theme as I walk you through my resume. I'm very passionate about gathering information and using it to solve puzzles.

"My first job was as a hostess in a diner. While I was there, I observed the operations, interviewed the employees, and found ways to reorganize the staff duties to make things more effective. I was promoted to assistant manager, where I implemented new processes that reduced wait times by 15% and improved customer satisfaction by 10%.

"Next, I went to Northern College, where I studied finance. While there, I worked as a research assistant for a college professor and for our admissions department. I gathered data about our admissions process, analyzed it, and found ways to reduce the application processing time by 30%.

"Currently, I'm working as a bookkeeper at Beacon Medical Devices, where I'm gathering and interpreting data about our business operations and marketing programs. Since I started, I've found ways to increase our company sales by over five million dollars and improve our marketing efficiency by 8%.

"I'm always looking to gather information and put it together in ways that can be used to improve a business. Now, I want to work in a role where I can pursue my passion for gathering information and using it to solve puzzles. I'm hoping that will be as a research analyst for your company."

Barbara looked down at her notepad and wrote a few notes. "Hmm. So tell me about a specific time when you used data to identify a business opportunity."

Lisa shifted in her seat as she thought about which S-T-A-R story might work best for this question.

"As a bookkeeper at Beacon Medical Supplies, one of my tasks is to find opportunities to help the company increase sales.

"To do this, I've researched various industry reports for medical supplies. I found one report that was full of data about sales trends for various categories. I noticed that sales for in-home testing kits were growing, and that's a category where we didn't have any offerings.

"Next, I conducted interviews with our sales team. Many of them said they would like to have in-home testing kits in our portfolio of products to sell. With their input, I was able to calculate the potential sales opportunity to be about five million dollars per year.

"Finally, I summarized my recommendation in a report for our executive team. I reviewed the report with my manager and gave her all the information she needed to present my recommendation at the next leadership team meeting.

"As a result, the executive team agreed to add in-home testing kits to our product portfolio. Next year, those products are forecasted to deliver over five million dollars in sales for our company."

Barbara nodded. "Nice. Now, if I were to ask you to recommend a new line of sporting goods for our company, how would you approach that?"

Lisa recognized this as a case question.

"My understanding is that you have a wide range of products for baseball and golf. For a new line of sporting goods, I'd use the approach I learned when I was a staff reporter for my college newspaper. It's the What, Who, Where, When, and Why approach.

"I'd start by understanding the 'What'—specifically, what other sports might be options. I'd use whatever data you have about the size and growth rates of various sporting goods categories. If you don't have a lot of data, I'd find industry reports that could provide the data. That would give me a list of potential categories to pursue.

"For the 'Who,' I'd want to know who your competitors and customers would be. I'd want to know how strong each competitor is in each category and how loyal their customers are. I could get this information from industry reports or by interviewing people who buy equipment for those sports.

"For the 'Where,' I'd want to know where equipment for those sports is sold. If it's primarily in brick-and-mortar stores, I'd want to gather information from the people who make buying decisions for those stores. If it's primarily online, I'd want to know who the biggest online retailers are for those sports and see what they wanted from a supplier.

"For the 'When,' I'd want to know when the retailers make decisions about the product lines they carry. Since most sports are seasonal, I'd want to formulate an offering for them before they make their seasonal buying decisions.

"Finally, for the 'Why,' I'd want to define why we could have a competitive advantage in each category. For example, if our suppliers who make golf equipment could also make equipment for another sport, we might be able to use our relationships with them to deliver a compelling offering for that other sport.

"I'd put all that information together in a recommendation that would show how we could enter various categories. That recommendation would include a prioritized list of potential categories, who our customers might be, where we would sell the products, when we would start offering them, and why customers would choose our products over our competition's products. That's how I'd approach building a recommendation for a new line of sporting goods."

Barbara wrote more notes on notepad. "Do you have any questions for me?"

Lisa picked up her pen and held it over her notepad. "Yes. What do you like most about working here?"

Barbara paused. "That's a good question. I guess it would have to be the sense of teamwork. Most of the people who work here have played sports while growing up. They're used to being part of a team, and I like that team environment."

Lisa smiled. "I know exactly what you mean. I played golf in high school. I really miss being part of a team like that. In fact, I forgot to mention that part of the reason I'm excited about working here is that I've been using your products for years. The clubs I used in high school were Premier. I'd love to work for a company that is part of those special times, like playing golf in high school was for me."

Barbara looked at her watch. "That's all the time we have. I'm going to take you to Mr. Baxter's office so you can interview with him now."

They both stood up. Barbara escorted Lisa to her next interview. Lisa spent the next hour sharing her P-E-N story with Mr. Baxter, telling a few of her S-T-A-R stories, and providing What-Who-Where-When-Why answers to a couple of case questions. At the end for their interview, Mr. Baxter called Barbara Gaines and asked her to come to his office to escort Lisa back to the lobby.

As they walked to the lobby, Barbara told Lisa to expect an email sometime in the next few weeks. They said goodbye, and Lisa walked out of the building feeling an immense sense of relief.

When Lisa got into her car, she let out a big sigh. She was exhausted. She felt like she had done well in the interviews, but was it enough?

The next two weeks were torture for Lisa. She received a few more rejection emails from other companies. She also had a few phone interviews with other potential employers. Nothing seemed to be showing any promise.

Finally, while she was in her cubicle working on a budget analysis, she received an email from Barbara Gaines. The subject line read: When can you start?

Lisa quickly read the email and went straight to Sandy's cubicle.

"Sandy, I got it. I got it."

Sandy looked up from her computer screen. "You got what?"

"The job at Premier Sporting Goods. I got it."

Sandy stood up and gave Lisa a big hug. "Of course you did. You'll be perfect for that job."

Review #5:
Nail Your Interviews

As you can see from Lisa's experience, interviews can be nerve-racking. No matter how much you prepare, the interview process can be inherently stressful. Lisa did a great job of making sure she was prepared.

In the Reference Materials section of this book, there's a checklist of things you should do before your interview. The list includes things like making sure your interviewing clothes are clean and pressed, getting plenty of rest the night before your interview, and showing up early on the day of your interview.

When your interviews start, let the recruiters set the pace. They may want to begin with small talk, they may want you to share a few things about yourself, or they may simply jump right into specific interview questions.

Remember to be calm and positive from the start of the interview all the way through to the end. Recruiters are looking for people who can be engaging and professional in any situation, so be friendly, but not too informal.

If interviewers ask you to tell them about yourself or walk them through your resume, you're in luck. You'll nail those questions since you've have practiced them so many times before.

If the interview starts with a different question, don't worry. You can adjust to any question they ask because you've done a great job preparing.

After you answer all the interview questions brilliantly, recruiters may ask, "Do you have any questions for me?" This is your opportunity to get them into selling mode. You want them to tell you why their organizations are great places to work.

When I'm interviewing candidates and they ask this type of question, I automatically start thinking about why that candidate would want to work for my company. Then, I start picturing them in my organization, and I respond by telling them why they should accept a job offer if I give them one.

That's it. That's the plan you'll need to get your career started. If you build a good job hunting strategy, customize your resumes for each opportunity, practice your interview skills, and nail your interviews, you'll be all set. It may seem like a lot, but just take it one step at a time and you'll be fine.

Remember, Lisa didn't know how to start. In fact, neither did I. Most of us, in the beginning, have no idea what we need to do to get great job. Fortunately, someone gave me the advice I've included in this book. I did what they said when I was interviewing, and I got job offers from all five of the top companies on my Job Hunting Tracker. While I can't promise you'll go five-for-five on your top choices, I can promise that you'll be better if you follow the advice in this book.

Most importantly, you should find a way to make job hunting and interview practice part of your routine. It's like anything else. If you have a good plan, you'll be off to a great start. If you dedicate time and effort to executing that plan, you'll become even better. This book gives you a good plan. The question is whether you'll dedicate the time and effort needed to become great.

CONCLUSION

Conclusion

Here's a summary of the game plan:

Step 1: Build Your Strategy. Before you start your job search, you should make sure you're looking for the right kind of job. Go online and read a variety of job descriptions to see which ones get you excited.

Once you're sure that you've chosen the right career path, start researching organizations that hire people in your field of interest. You can do this with the help of online sites that have a variety of job listings. You can also talk with friends and family members, who may have information about the types of jobs you want.

As you evaluate potential employers, start categorizing them into tiers. Your top tier will include employers that are the best fits for your professional and personal goals. Other potential employers can be included in your second tier or your list of safety companies. If you can't get into your top-tier choices, the other companies might still be good places to start the next phase of your career.

As you identify potential employers, use your Job Hunting Tracker to record notes about each job. Also, make sure you find job descriptions from your top-tier employers. Those job descriptions will be your cheat sheets as you polish your resume and practice your interview skills.

Step 2: Customize Your Resume. The secret to a good resume is using a job description to customize it. Your resume should include any experience you have that relates to the job description for the opportunity you want.

For each experience you put on your resume, list the actions you've taken and the results you've gotten that are most like those on the job description. Recruiters are looking for people whose experiences line up with the role they're hiring for. As such, make sure your resume lines up, as closely as possible, with the recruiters' job descriptions.

Also, remember to include a few eye-catching interests at the bottom of your resume. Those interests may entice a recruiter to add you to their interview list, perhaps because they have something in common with you or they're curious about something you've done.

Step 3: Practice for Opening Questions. This is the easiest step in the process. Since most recruiters ask the same types of opening questions, you can start with the list of interview questions on my website. Just go to AmazingJobSkills.com and download the questions. You can find them by clicking on the "Templates" link in the menu at the top of the home page.

There are hundreds of books that include lists of interview questions. My favorite is *Amazing Interview Answers* by yours truly. Yes, I am biased. However, I won't be offended if you use other sources to get your list of interview questions, as long as you have a good list to work with.

For most opening questions, I recommend you use the P-E-N framework to tell the recruiter what you're passionate about, what relevant experiences you have, and what you want to do next. Make sure your passion, experiences, and next steps line up with the job you want.

Remember, recruiters are trying to find people who will love working for their organizations. Therefore, when you're practicing for this question, look at the recruiter's job description and tell them why you'll be passionate about doing the tasks on that job description.

Step 4: Practice for Fit Questions. When recruiters ask you fit questions, you should be ready with a variety of good stories about yourself that use the S-T-A-R framework. That means you should be ready to describe your experiences that highlight situations, tasks, actions, and results related to what the recruiter is asking about.

I recommend that you start with your four or five biggest accomplishments. For each of them, write down one sentence that describes the situation, which could include your job title and the organization you were in. Then, write down your task, which could be the assignment or goal you had. Then, list the two or three actions you took to accomplish that task. Finally, write down the result you got, and try to state that result in a way that's as measurable as possible.

This S-T-A-R technique will make your answer interesting for recruiters, since it will give them a story about you that has a beginning, a middle, and an end. It will also show them that you can work towards a goal, take necessary actions, and get meaningful results.

You should choose S-T-A-R stories from your past that highlight the type of work you want to do. If you're in a creative field, practice telling stories about the times you've delivered creative results. If you're in an analytical field, your stories should highlight your analytical skills.

Step 5: Practice for Case Questions. This is the trickiest part of the process. Since case questions are different for every type of career field, you'll have to do a little extra research to develop good answers to these questions.

Currently, there are a variety of books available about case questions for technology, consulting, education, and healthcare jobs. If you're in another field, you might need to look harder to find good questions. I've included a few case questions in my *Amazing Interview Answers* book, but you'll likely need more if you're in a case-oriented field. Once you get a good list of questions, practice your answers with other people in your career field.

Step 6: Nail Your Interviews. The final step of the process is to nail your interviews. Most employers use the interviews as the primary factor when considering candidates for jobs. Sure, a good resume or a compelling cover letter might get you into an interview, but it's the interview itself that will determine whether you get a job offer.

As such, make sure you're well rested and prepared for your interviews. When you show up on your interview day, you should be dressed appropriately and ready to dazzle the recruiter.

The best way to perform well in interviews is to have plenty of practice ahead of time. Remember, if your priority is to get a good job, you should commit the time and effort needed to prepare. This book gives you the game plan. You just need to execute that plan.

That's all you need to get started. Now, start researching the types of jobs you want and follow the process I've described in this book.

Best wishes as you begin the next phase of your career.

I do have one final request. Please take a minute to rate this book on the site where you bought it and write a review to tell others what you think. Your review will really help to raise awareness of the book. Furthermore, please consider telling a job-hunting friend about what you've learned.

REFERENCE MATERIALS

Reference Materials

REFERENCE MATERIALS

Job Hunting Tracker

Use this section of the book to prepare your job-hunting strategy and complete your Job Hunting Tracker.

Enter your criteria for the type of job you want:

1. _____

2. _____

3. _____

4. _____

Examples:
- flexible work schedule
- geography (close to a specific location)
- pay above a certain level (over $_____ per hour or per year)
- working with numbers
- requires creativity, problem solving, organizational skills, etc.

Potential Career Paths:

Job Title: _____

Primary Duties: _____

_____

_____

_____

Job Title: _____

Primary Duties: _____

_____

_____

_____

Job Hunting Tracker

Company #1: _____

Job Title: _____

Listing Location (Job Site) and/or Recruiter Contact Info: _____

_____

Job Description, Key Responsibilities, and/or Qualifications: _____

_____

Comments: _____

Tier (Top, Middle, or Bottom): _____

Date Application/Resume Submitted: _____

Date(s) of Subsequent Communications: _____

Date(s) of Interview: _____

Date(s) Follow-Up Communications Sent: _____

Company #2: _____

Job Title: _____

Listing Location (Job Site) and/or Recruiter Contact Info: _____

_____

Job Description, Key Responsibilities, and/or Qualifications: _____

_____

Comments: _____

Tier (Top, Middle, or Bottom): _____

Date Application/Resume Submitted: _____

Date(s) of Subsequent Communications: _____

Date(s) of Interview: _____

Date(s) Follow-Up Communications Sent: _____

AMAZING JOB SEARCH GAMEPLAN

Job Hunting Tracker (continued)

Company #3: _____

Job Title: _____

Listing Location (Job Site) and/or Recruiter Contact Info: _____

_____

Job Description, Key Responsibilities, and/or Qualifications: _____

_____

Comments: _____

Tier (Top, Middle, or Bottom): _____

Date Application/Resume Submitted: _____

Date(s) of Subsequent Communications: _____

Date(s) of Interview: _____

Date(s) Follow-Up Communications Sent: _____

Company #4: _____

Job Title: _____

Listing Location (Job Site) and/or Recruiter Contact Info: _____

_____

Job Description, Key Responsibilities, and/or Qualifications: _____

_____

Comments: _____

Tier (Top, Middle, or Bottom): _____

Date Application/Resume Submitted: _____

Date(s) of Subsequent Communications: _____

Date(s) of Interview: _____

Date(s) Follow-Up Communications Sent: _____

Job Hunting Tracker (continued)

Company #5: _____

Job Title: _____

Listing Location (Job Site) and/or Recruiter Contact Info: _____

_____

Job Description, Key Responsibilities, and/or Qualifications: _____

_____

Comments: _____

Tier (Top, Middle, or Bottom): _____

Date Application/Resume Submitted: _____

Date(s) of Subsequent Communications: _____

Date(s) of Interview: _____

Date(s) Follow-Up Communications Sent: _____

Company #6: _____

Job Title: _____

Listing Location (Job Site) and/or Recruiter Contact Info: _____

_____

Job Description, Key Responsibilities, and/or Qualifications: _____

_____

Comments: _____

Tier (Top, Middle, or Bottom): _____

Date Application/Resume Submitted: _____

Date(s) of Subsequent Communications: _____

Date(s) of Interview: _____

Date(s) Follow-Up Communications Sent: _____

Job Hunting Tracker (continued)

Company #7: _____

Job Title: _____

Listing Location (Job Site) and/or Recruiter Contact Info: _____

_____

Job Description, Key Responsibilities, and/or Qualifications: _____

_____

Comments: _____

Tier (Top, Middle, or Bottom): _____

Date Application/Resume Submitted: _____

Date(s) of Subsequent Communications: _____

Date(s) of Interview: _____

Date(s) Follow-Up Communications Sent: _____

Company #8: _____

Job Title: _____

Listing Location (Job Site) and/or Recruiter Contact Info: _____

_____

Job Description, Key Responsibilities, and/or Qualifications: _____

_____

Comments: _____

Tier (Top, Middle, or Bottom): _____

Date Application/Resume Submitted: _____

Date(s) of Subsequent Communications: _____

Date(s) of Interview: _____

Date(s) Follow-Up Communications Sent: _____

Job Hunting Tracker (continued)

Company #9: _____

Job Title: _____

Listing Location (Job Site) and/or Recruiter Contact Info: _____

_____

Job Description, Key Responsibilities, and/or Qualifications: _____

_____

Comments: _____

Tier (Top, Middle, or Bottom): _____

Date Application/Resume Submitted: _____

Date(s) of Subsequent Communications: _____

Date(s) of Interview: _____

Date(s) Follow-Up Communications Sent: _____

Company #10: _____

Job Title: _____

Listing Location (Job Site) and/or Recruiter Contact Info: _____

_____

Job Description, Key Responsibilities, and/or Qualifications: _____

_____

Comments: _____

Tier (Top, Middle, or Bottom): _____

Date Application/Resume Submitted: _____

Date(s) of Subsequent Communications: _____

Date(s) of Interview: _____

Date(s) Follow-Up Communications Sent: _____

Job Hunting Tracker (continued)

Company #11: _____

Job Title: _____

Listing Location (Job Site) and/or Recruiter Contact Info: _____

_____

Job Description, Key Responsibilities, and/or Qualifications: _____

_____

Comments: _____

Tier (Top, Middle, or Bottom): _____

Date Application/Resume Submitted: _____

Date(s) of Subsequent Communications: _____

Date(s) of Interview: _____

Date(s) Follow-Up Communications Sent: _____

Company #12: _____

Job Title: _____

Listing Location (Job Site) and/or Recruiter Contact Info: _____

_____

Job Description, Key Responsibilities, and/or Qualifications: _____

_____

Comments: _____

Tier (Top, Middle, or Bottom): _____

Date Application/Resume Submitted: _____

Date(s) of Subsequent Communications: _____

Date(s) of Interview: _____

Date(s) Follow-Up Communications Sent: _____

Job Hunting Tracker (continued)

Company #13: _____

Job Title: _____

Listing Location (Job Site) and/or Recruiter Contact Info: _____

_____

Job Description, Key Responsibilities, and/or Qualifications: _____

_____

Comments: _____

Tier (Top, Middle, or Bottom): _____

Date Application/Resume Submitted: _____

Date(s) of Subsequent Communications: _____

Date(s) of Interview: _____

Date(s) Follow-Up Communications Sent: _____

Company #14: _____

Job Title: _____

Listing Location (Job Site) and/or Recruiter Contact Info: _____

_____

Job Description, Key Responsibilities, and/or Qualifications: _____

_____

Comments: _____

Tier (Top, Middle, or Bottom): _____

Date Application/Resume Submitted: _____

Date(s) of Subsequent Communications: _____

Date(s) of Interview: _____

Date(s) Follow-Up Communications Sent: _____

Job Hunting Tracker (continued)

Company #15: _____

Job Title: _____

Listing Location (Job Site) and/or Recruiter Contact Info: _____

_____

Job Description, Key Responsibilities, and/or Qualifications: _____

_____

Comments: _____

Tier (Top, Middle, or Bottom): _____

Date Application/Resume Submitted: _____

Date(s) of Subsequent Communications: _____

Date(s) of Interview: _____

Date(s) Follow-Up Communications Sent: _____

Company #16: _____

Job Title: _____

Listing Location (Job Site) and/or Recruiter Contact Info: _____

_____

Job Description, Key Responsibilities, and/or Qualifications: _____

_____

Comments: _____

Tier (Top, Middle, or Bottom): _____

Date Application/Resume Submitted: _____

Date(s) of Subsequent Communications: _____

Date(s) of Interview: _____

Date(s) Follow-Up Communications Sent: _____

Job Hunting Tracker (continued)

Company #17: _____

Job Title: _____

Listing Location (Job Site) and/or Recruiter Contact Info: _____

_____

Job Description, Key Responsibilities, and/or Qualifications: _____

_____

Comments: _____

Tier (Top, Middle, or Bottom):   _____

Date Application/Resume Submitted: _____

Date(s) of Subsequent Communications: _____

Date(s) of Interview: _____

Date(s) Follow-Up Communications Sent: _____

Company #18: _____

Job Title: _____

Listing Location (Job Site) and/or Recruiter Contact Info: _____

_____

Job Description, Key Responsibilities, and/or Qualifications: _____

_____

Comments: _____

Tier (Top, Middle, or Bottom):   _____

Date Application/Resume Submitted: _____

Date(s) of Subsequent Communications: _____

Date(s) of Interview: _____

Date(s) Follow-Up Communications Sent: _____

Job Hunting Tracker (continued)

Company #19: _____

Job Title: _____

Listing Location (Job Site) and/or Recruiter Contact Info: _____

_____

Job Description, Key Responsibilities, and/or Qualifications: _____

_____

Comments: _____

Tier (Top, Middle, or Bottom): _____

Date Application/Resume Submitted: _____

Date(s) of Subsequent Communications: _____

Date(s) of Interview: _____

Date(s) Follow-Up Communications Sent: _____

Company #20: _____

Job Title: _____

Listing Location (Job Site) and/or Recruiter Contact Info: _____

_____

Job Description, Key Responsibilities, and/or Qualifications: _____

_____

Comments: _____

Tier (Top, Middle, or Bottom): _____

Date Application/Resume Submitted: _____

Date(s) of Subsequent Communications: _____

Date(s) of Interview: _____

Date(s) Follow-Up Communications Sent: _____

Resume Tools & Examples

This section includes tools for you to use to build your resume. Start by writing the job duties and skills required as listed on the job descriptions of your top-tier job prospects.

Job duties:

_____

_____

_____

_____

_____

_____

_____

_____

_____

Skills required:

_____

_____

_____

_____

_____

Fill in the information below. Make sure you include any experiences you have that are related to the job duties listed on the previous page.

Resume Template

Your Name: _____

Street Address: _____

Email address: _____

phone number: _____

EDUCATION

UNIVERSITY NAME: _____

City, State: _____

Degree: _____

Graduation Date (or Anticipated Graduation Date): _____

School Activities, Offices Held, Honors, or Major Awards: _____

_____

_____

_____

_____

EXPERIENCE

EMPLOYER NAME (most recent): _____

Time Period Worked (example: 2017 - 2018): _____

Job Title (most recent): _____

- Action and result: _____

  _____

- Action and result: _____

  _____

- Action and result: _____

  _____

EMPLOYER NAME: _____

Time Period Worked (example: 2015 - 2016): _____

Job Title (most recent): _____

- Action and result: _____

  _____

- Action and result: _____

  _____

- Action and result: _____

  _____

EMPLOYER NAME: _____

Time Period Worked (example: 2013 - 2014): _____

Job Title (most recent): _____

- Action and result: _____

  _____

- Action and result: _____

  _____

- Action and result: _____

  _____

ADDITIONAL INFORMATION

Major awards, volunteer positions, and interests

- _____

  _____

- _____

  _____

- _____

  _____

In a word processing program, type the content that you've written on the previous pages into a resume using the following format. For an electronic copy of this template, go to www.AmazingJobSkills.com, and download the "Resume Template" file in the "Templates" section of the site.

Name
Street Address
email address, phone number

EDUCATION
UNIVERSITY NAME   **City, State**
Degree   Anticipated Graduation Date
- School Activities and/or Offices Held
- Honors and/or Major Awards

EXPERIENCE
EMPLOYER NAME (most recent)   **City, State**
Job Title (most recent)   Years Worked
- Action and result
- Action and result
- Action and result

EMPLOYER NAME   City, State
Job Title   Years Worked
- Action and result
- Action and result
- Action and result

EMPLOYER NAME   City, State
Job Title   Years Worked
- Action and result
- Action and result
- Action and result

ADDITIONAL INFORMATION
- Major awards
- Volunteer positions
- Interest

This section of the book includes examples of job descriptions and resumes that are customized based on specific duties in those job descriptions.

On each job description, key words are outlined. You can see how those key words are included on the resume examples. This illustrates how you can use job descriptions to customize your resume for each position you are applying for.

Near the end of this section of the book, there's a place for you to enter the job description details for positions that you want. There is also a blank resume template for you to use for taking notes related to your resume.

Sample Job Description

Research Assistant

Job duties:

- Gather data about consumers, competitors, and market conditions
- Interpret data and make recommendations to improve businesses
- Identify opportunities to increase company sales and efficiency
- Conduct interviews and analyze responses
- Prepared reports that summarized research

Skills required:
- Investigative skills
- Ability to recognize patterns in data
- Ability to solve puzzles using incomplete information
- Ability to deal with ambiguity
- Ability to summarize complex information into simple proposals

For more job descriptions, see www.bls.gov/ooh

Lisa Brimmer

985 8th Street, Apt 23, Cleveland, Ohio 44101
l.brimmer@mymail.com, 216-555-8743

EDUCATION

NORTHERN COLLEGE   Cleveland, OH
Associated Degree in Finance   May 2017
- Staff Writer, Northern College Newspaper
- Chapter Secretary, Alpha Gamma Beta sorority

EXPERIENCE

BEACON MEDICAL DEVICES   Cleveland, OH
Bookkeeper   2017 - present
- Gather data about consumers, competitors, and market conditions
- Interpret data and make recommendations to improve business strategies, operating efficiency, and marketing plans
- Identified opportunities to increase company sales by over $5MM
- Identified savings opportunities that reduced overhead by $200K

NORTHERN COLLEGE   Cleveland, OH
Research Assistant   2016 - 2017
- Conducted interviews and analyzed data for college marketing class
- Prepared reports that summarized research; made recommendations to professor that were included in four published articles

MAIN STREET DINER   Littleton, OH
Hostess and Assistant Manager   2013 - 2016
- Greeted guests and ensured excellent dining experiences
- Identified and implemented initiatives that reduced guest wait times by 15% during busiest business hours
- Supervised wait staff and implemented processes to improve guest satisfaction by 10%

ADDITIONAL INFORMATION

- Freelance researcher and writer for blogs about sporting events
- Captain of the Littleton High School cross-country team
- Interests include running, Sudoku, and writing blog articles

Sample Job Description

Bookkeeper

Job duties:
- Prepare sales trackers and forecasts
- Manage budgets and prepare financial reports
- Analyze data
- Evaluate profitability of financial transactions
- Record financial transactions

Skills required:
- Attention to detail
- Strong analytical and math skills
- Strong organizational skills
- Strong computer skills, particularly with spreadsheets and financial software

For more job descriptions, see www.bls.gov/ooh

Sandy Garcia

1212 Suburban Lane, Cleveland, OH 44101
sandy-g@mailemail.com, 843-555-7654

EDUCATION

COLUMBUS COLLEGE   Great Lake, MT
Associates Degree in Business Administration   May 2007
- Treasurer, Women's Business Club
- Membership Committee Chair, Campus Charity Organization

EXPERIENCE

EAGLE CRAFT STORES   Cleveland, OH
Marketing Analyst   2010 - 2015
- Prepared sales trackers and forecasts for team of 15 marketers
- Managed budget and identified efficiencies that delivered $40,000 in costs savings
- Analyzed data and developed recommendations resulting in 20% improvement in marketing impact with no additional cost

Assistant Marketing Analyst   2007 - 2010
- Prepared sales trackers and forecasts for team of 6 marketers
- Managed budget and identified efficiencies that delivered $15,000 in costs savings
- Evaluated profitability of product lines and identified promotional strategy improvements resulting in 5% increase in sales and 3% increase in margin

BLACK DIAMOND RESORT   Black Diamond, MT
Financial Analyst   Summer 2006
- Recorded financial transactions for company that owned 5 retail stores
- Evaluated profitability of product lines and identified efficiencies that reduced overhead costs by $10,000

ADDITIONAL INFORMATION

- Volunteer, Cleveland Philanthropic Society
- Earned Eagle Craft Stores Employee of the Month Award 4 times
- Interests include reading historical fiction, playing trivia games, and cooking

Sample Job Description

Marketing Manager

Job duties:
- Analyze data to identify opportunities for new products
- Conduct research and build business plans to increase sales
- Lead cross-functional teams to develop new marketing campaigns
- Lead agency partners to develop marketing and sales materials
- Manage timelines and budgets

Skills required:
- Analytical skills
- Problem solving skills
- Leadership skills
- Communication skills
- Creative skills

For more job descriptions, see www.bls.gov/ooh

Jim Harrison

32 College Avenue, Apt 3B, Center City, SC 29910
j.harrison@southernstate.edu, 843-555-1212

EDUCATION

SOUTHERN STATE UNIVERSITY   Center City, SC
Bachelor of Business Administration   May 2016
- Communication Committee Chair, Debate Team
- Varsity Track Team, 400m Hurdles and 4x400 Relay

EXPERIENCE

SIZZLE MARKETING   Lufton, SC
Marketing Manager   2016 - present
- Analyzed data from competitive camps to identify new activities
- Conducted research among camp attendees and parents; developed marketing campaign projected to increase applications by 40%
- Led cross-functional team of counselors, activity directors, and foodservice managers to develop online strategy that delivered 50% increase in site traffic

HILLSIDE EXPLORERS CAMP   Woodlands Village, SC
Assistant Marketing Director   2015 - 2017
- Led agency partners to develop camp's first-ever social media site and direct mail campaign that generated 30% increase in applications
- Managed timelines and budgets for three new camp activities
- Instructed 40 students on survival skills and fitness activities

SPEEDY CAR RENTAL   Tinytown, SC
Sales Representative   Summer 2014
- Interview customers and determine best services to meet their needs
- Designed campaign that delivered 20% increase in online sales
- Conducted market research on competitive pricing strategies

ADDITIONAL INFORMATION

- Webmaster for Center City Running Club website (crc.run.club)
- Interests include running marathons, reading psychological thriller books, and producing YouTube videos

Sample Job Description

Teaching Assistant

Job duties:
- Tutor students who need extra help
- Assist teachers with lesson planning
- Grade assignments and exams
- Maintain order in classrooms
- Prepare written evaluations summarizing abilities for students

Skills required:
- Communication skills
- Patience
- Ability to explain complex concepts in simple terms
- Ability to adapt to challenging situations
- Strong listening skills

For more job descriptions, see www.bls.gov/ooh

William Jackson

985 8th Street, Apt 23, Center City, SC 29910
w.jackson@southernstate.edu, 843-555-8743

EDUCATION

SOUTHERN STATE UNIVERSITY Center City, SC
Bachelor of Science in Education May 2017
- Career Counselor, Office of Career Development
- VP of Communications, Education Club

EXPERIENCE

MIDDLEVILLE HIGH SCHOOL Middleville, SC
Teaching Assistant 2017 - present
- Tutored over 40 students in algebra and geometry
- Assisted teachers with lesson plans for 8 classes
- Graded assignments and exams for over 200 students
- Assisted head coaches for basketball and track teams

HILLSIDE EXPLORERS CAMP Woodlands Village, SC
Senior Camp Counselor Summer 2016
- Tutored 25 camp attendees to improve writing and crafts skills
- Assisted camp director with lesson planning for 5 camp activities
- Maintained order among 60+ teenage students during classroom sessions and outdoor training exercises

Camp Counselor Summer 2016
- Graded tests and writing assignments for over 50 camp attendees
- Helped maintain order among 30+ teenage students during classroom sessions and outdoor training exercises
- Prepared written evaluations to communicate progress to students and parents

ADDITIONAL INFORMATION

- Volunteer and basketball coach at Boys & Girls Club
- Winner of Middleton High School talent contest
- Interests include basketball, chess, and collecting rare books

Sample Job Description

Nurse

Job duties:
- Measure vital signs for patients
- Record medical histories and health concerns
- Assist patients with moving about the facility
- Observe and record changes in patients' conditions
- Feed, bathe, and dress patients

Skills required:
- Compassion
- Resilience
- Strong communication skills
- Teamwork and people skills
- Medical knowledge

For more job descriptions, see www.bls.gov/ooh

Sarah Barker

219 Center Street, Center City, SC 29910
s.barker@southernstate.edu, 843-444-2323

EDUCATION

SOUTHERN STATE UNIVERSITY   Center City, SC
Bachelor of Science, Nursing & Psychology   May 2015
- Vice President, Student Healthcare Organization
- Member, Campus Speech Club

EXPERIENCE

CENTER CITY HOSPITAL   Center City, SC
Nursing Assistant   2015 - present
- Measured vital signs for over 200 patients
- Recorded medical histories and health concerns for over 350 patients
- Trained 15 nurses and medical assistants on new software for recording medical records; saved company $10,000 in training costs
- Designed and implemented new check-in process that reduced waiting times by 30%

PLEASANTON RETIREMENT HOME   Pleasanton, WI
Orderly   2012 - 2014
- Assisted patients with moving around facility, including pushing wheelchairs and taking patients for walks
- Observed and recorded changes in physical and mental conditions of patients
- Recognized as Employee of the Month for receiving top scores on surveys completed by patients and family members

SUNNYVILLE HOSPITAL GIFT SHOP   Sunnyville, WI
Cashier   Summer 2011
- Assisted customers in making purchase decisions
- Answered customer questions about store products

ADDITIONAL INFORMATION

- Volunteer, Hearts for Children charity
- Interests include travel, cooking, and tennis
- Fluent in English, Spanish, and French

Sample Job Description

Engineering

Job duties:
- Develop engineering plans and designs for structures and systems
- Conduct inspections and tests to ensure the quality of construction
- Prepare budgets and identify cost saving opportunities
- Write reports to recommend engineering solutions
- Conduct research and provide technical assistance to engineers

Skills required:
- Problem solving skills
- Communication skills
- Analytical and math skills
- Teamwork and people skills
- Technical engineering knowledge

For more job descriptions, see www.bls.gov/ooh

Abby Walker

915 Highland Circle, Apt 22, Center City, SC 29910
a.walker@southernstate.edu, 843-333-9876

EDUCATION

EASTERN UNIVERSITY   Pineville, PA
Masters of Science in Engineering   Anticipated Graduation May 2019
- GPA: 3.85
- Treasurer, Engineering Club

SOUTHERN STATE UNIVERSITY   Center City, SC
Bachelor of Science in Mathematics   May 2014
- Member, Physics Club
- Staff Reporter, Newsy News school newspaper

EXPERIENCE

UNIVERSITY CITY ANIMAL SHELTER   Center City, SC
Assistant Office Manager   2014 - 2017
- Developed engineering plans for new kennel system that gives each animal 30% more living space within existing building structure
- Conducted inspections and tests to ensure new kennel system will be structurally sound
- Prepared budgets and identified cost savings measures that reduce cost of new kennel system by over $20,000

HOMES FOR HUMANS VOLUNTEER   Middleton, TX
Summer Construction Volunteer   Summer 2013
- Wrote reports to recommend construction techniques improvements that are projected to reduce future home maintenance cost by 20%
- Conducted research on building materials and identified higher-quality options that would reduce material costs by 20%
- Performed inspections to ensure building structures met specifications

ADDITIONAL INFORMATION

- Volunteer, Unity Church Audio/Visual Team
- Winner of Centerville High School Science Fair with project titled "Stronger Construction Designs for Bridges"
- Interests include robotics and martial arts (black belt in taekwondo)

Sample Job Description

Computer Program

Job duties:

- Code, test, and debug programming for software applications
- Analyze and recommend improvements to computer networks
- Identify and repair technical issues
- Install and trouble-shoot computer hardware and software
- Address technical support requests from employees

Skills required:

- Problem solving skills
- Creative skills
- Analytical and math skills
- Teamwork and people skills
- Technical computer knowledge

For more job descriptions, see www.bls.gov/ooh

Ethan Wright

708 L Street, Anchor Point, AK 99501
e.wright@northernstate.edu, 907-444-2468

EDUCATION

NORTHERN STATE UNIVERSITY   Anchor Point, AK
Bachelor of Science in Computer Science   May 2013
- Winner, Computer Club's Annual Programming Competition
- Founding Member, Electronic Game Developers Society

EXPERIENCE

BIGBOX ELECTRONICS STORE   Anchor Point, AK
Computer Programming Technician   2015 - present
- Coded, tested, and debugged software applications used by over 500 employees to record sales and track inventory
- Analyzed and installed improvements to computer networks that reduced downtimes by an average of 80%
- Identified and repaired technical issues with existing software applications to improve system efficiency by over 20%

Computer Repair Technician   2013 - 2015
- Installed and ensured proper functioning of computer hardware and software for over 100 customers
- Addressed over 50 technical support requests from customers
- Led 4 training sessions on new computer software applications for employees and customers

GIGAPLEX GAME DEVELOPERS   Fairshores, AK
Computer Game Development Intern   Summer 2012
- Installed and ensured proper functioning of computer hardware and software for over 100 customers
- Addressed over 50 technical support requests from employees

ADDITIONAL INFORMATION

- Volunteer troop leader for Boy Scouts of America
- Eagle Scout: final project involved designing and installing a new computer network for Franklin High School in Greentown, SC
- Interests include blog writing, photography, and playing the guitar

Sample Job Description

Sales Person

Job duties:

- Build relationships with customers
- Recommend products or services based on customer needs
- Inform customers of sales, promotions, and policies
- Demonstrate or explain how products and services work
- Answer customer questions or disputes

Skills required:

- Problem solving skills
- Creative skills
- Analytical and math skills
- Teamwork and people skills
- Technical computer knowledge

For more job descriptions, see www.bls.gov/ooh

Thomas Bailey

394 Colter Street, Red Hills, CA 92320
tombailey1@mailemail.com, 909-444-2468

EDUCATION

RED HILLS HIGH SCHOOL   Red Hills, CA
Senior   Anticipated Graduation May 2019
- GPA: 3.1
- Relevant Coursework: Public Speaking, Spanish, Journalism
- Clubs: Student Council, Drama Club
- Athletics: Varsity Basketball, JV Track & Field

EXPERIENCE

RED HILLS HIGH SCHOOL YEARBOOK   Red Hills, CA
Editor   2018 - present
- Built relationships with art professors; leveraged art students to take yearbook photos; resulted in $5,000 reduction in photography costs
- Recommended advertising solutions to local vendors that delivered incremental $10,000 revenue source for yearbook
- Informed customers of discount programs for pre-purchasing yearbooks resulting in 5% increase in sales

FREE SAMPLES TEMP AGENCY   Red Hills, CA
Sampling Event Staff Member   Summer 2018
- Demonstrated and explained how to use cooking ingredients and cleaning supplies
- Answered customer questions about featured products

RED HILLS HIGH SCHOOL FOOTBALL TEAM   2016 - 2018
Equipment Manager
- Built relationships with coaches and athletes
- Recommended sports equipment based on needs of athletes
- Demonstrated proper use of equipment to over 40 players

ADDITIONAL INFORMATION

- Winner of Red Hills High School Annual Debate Competition
- Interests include writing, graphic design, and board games

Sample Job Description

Cashier

Job duties:

- Greet customers
- Scan purchases
- Accept payment, make change, and provide receipts
- Monitor store to ensure security of merchandise
- Answer customer questions and provide information as requested

Skills required:

- Problem solving skills
- Creative skills
- Analytical and math skills
- Teamwork and people skills
- Technical computer knowledge

For more job descriptions, see www.bls.gov/ooh

Teresa Martin

1512 9th Avenue, Denton, MI 48430
teresamartin394@dentonisd.edu, 248-555-0099

EDUCATION

DENTON HIGH SCHOOL   Denton, MI
Junior   Anticipated Graduation May 2020

- GPA: 3.3
- Relevant Coursework: Calculus, Business Management
- Clubs: Pep Squad, Band

EXPERIENCE

GROVER'S CORNER STORE   Denton, MI
Cashier   Summer 2018

- Greeted customers and ensured they felt welcome
- Scanned purchases for merchandise
- Accepted payment, made change, and provided receipts
- Selected as employee of the month for July 2018

DENTON MUNICIPLE POOL   Denton, MI
Lifeguard   Summer 2017

- Monitor pool-related activities to ensure safety of swimmers and security of facility
- Answered customer questions and provided information as requested
- Provided swim lessons to 10 children age 4 through 8

SELF-EMPLOYED   Denton, MI
Baby Sitter   2015 - 2017

- Supervised children age 2 through 5
- Played games and disciplined children as needed

ADDITIONAL INFORMATION

- Volunteer troop leader for Boy Scouts of America
- Interests include playing clarinet, reading historical fiction, and watching old movies

SAMPLE INTERVIEW ANSWERS

Sample Interview Questions

SAMPLE INTERVIEW ANSWERS

This section includes a list of common interview questions.

Opening Questions

1. Can you tell me about yourself?
2. Will you walk me through your resume?
3. What makes you a good choice for this job?
4. Why are you interested in this job?
5. Why should I hire you?
6. Where do you see yourself in five years?
7. Can you describe your dream job?
8. Why do you want to leave your current job?
9. What do you know about our organization?
10. What do you know about the job you're applying for?

Fit Questions

1. What is your biggest strength?
2. What is your biggest weakness?
3. Can you tell me about a time when you've demonstrated creativity?
4. Can you tell me about your leadership style?
5. How would a friend describe you?
6. Will you tell me about your biggest achievement?
7. Can you tell me about a time when you've demonstrated leadership?
8. Can you tell me about a time when you've demonstrated analytical skills?
9. Can you tell me about a time when you've demonstrated persistence?
10. Can you tell me about a time when you've demonstrated collaboration?

Case Questions

Case questions are specific to particular career fields. As such, here are examples of case questions for a few common types of jobs:

Business Case Questions:

1. If your brand's sales start to decline, what questions would you ask?
2. You discover that some of your products are defective. What do you do?
3. You have to make a decision between investing in advertising, reducing your prices, or improving your product quality. How do you make that decision?
4. How would you determine the size of the market for a specific type of product?

Education Case Questions:

1. If you had a disruptive student in your class, what would you do?
2. How would you handle a parent who wants constant updates on their child's progress?
3. How would you teach a child to add fractions, if they didn't understand how to do it?
4. If you had to design a new lesson plan for your favorite subject, how would you do it?

Healthcare Case Questions:

1. You have a patient who faints. What do you do?
2. Can you list the risk factors related to diabetes?
3. What is your favorite medication, and why?
4. How would you address a patient who is experiencing a sudden drop in blood pressure?

Engineering Case Questions:

1. If I asked you to design a new highway intersection, how would you approach that?
2. If I asked you to assess the strength of a metal beam, how would you do that?
3. What would you do if we asked you to design a bowling alley for blind people?
4. How many golf balls would fit in this room?

Computer Science Case Questions:

1. If your boss asked you to debug a software program, how would you approach it?
2. If you had to redesign a computer network to handle ten times as many users, what would you do?
3. If you had to create an app with five other people, how would you divide the work?
4. If you had to fix a computer network that was experiencing 5% downtime, how would you do that?

SAMPLE INTERVIEW ANSWERS

Sample Interview Answers

This section includes several commonly asked opening questions, a great answer for each question, and templates for you to jot down a few notes concerning your unique answer. Review the sample answers, and then write your answer to each question based on your own personal experiences and skills.

Opening Question #1:

Sample question: Can you tell me about yourself?

Sample answer for someone seeking a marketing job:

"I've always been passionate about figuring out what motivates people.

"For the past two summers, I worked as a camp counselor, which gave me many opportunities to get better understanding what motivates people. During my first summer there, I redesigned our camp's website. I interviewed kids and parents to see what influenced them to choose specific summer camps, and I built a site that helped generate a 30% increase in applications. The next summer, I was promoted to the position of Camp Communications Manager. I loved that job because it gave me additional opportunities to figure out what motivated parents and kids to choose summer camps. I conducted research and built a marketing strategy that's projected to increase applications by another 40%.

"Now I'm looking for a position where I can use my passion for motivating people to build compelling marketing campaigns. I'm hoping it will be with your company."

AMAZING JOB SEARCH GAMEPLAN

Write your answer to this question here.

PASSION: _____

_____

_____

EXPERIENCE: _____

_____

_____

_____

_____

_____

_____

_____

_____

_____

NEXT: _____

_____

_____

_____

_____

Opening Question #2:

Sample question: Can you walk me through your resume?

Sample answer for someone seeking a nursing job:

"As I walk you through my resume, I'll highlight a theme, which is my passion for helping people.

"Going chronologically from the bottom of my resume upwards, you'll see that my interests include foreign languages and travel. I've always enjoyed those things because they help me understand people from different backgrounds.

"My first volunteer experience was with an organization called Hearts for Children. That's where I became interested in healthcare. I really admired the way the nurses and psychologists helped kids who were dealing with illnesses. Since then, I've had two summer jobs that I've absolutely loved. The first was as an orderly at a retirement home where I did everything from feeding patients to helping them get around the facilities. The second was as a nursing assistant at a big medical center. In addition to performing my regular duties, I learned a new software program they were installing, and I trained fifteen nurses on the program. You'll also see that I'm getting a dual degree in nursing and psychology, which should help me pursue my passion for helping people.

"Now I'm looking for a position where I can help people while they're being treated at medical facilities. Based on my research, I think your organization will be a great place for me to do that."

Write your answer to this question here.

PASSION: _____

_____

_____

EXPERIENCE: _____

_____

_____

_____

_____

_____

_____

_____

_____

_____

NEXT: _____

_____

_____

_____

_____

Opening Question #3:

Sample question: Why are you a good choice for this job?

Sample answer for someone seeking an engineering job:

"I'm a good choice because of my passion for solving complicated problems. From what I read in the job description for this position, it looks like you want someone who can solve a variety of complicated problems including developing engineering plans, conducting inspections, and preparing budgets. Here's what makes me good at these things.

"I take a very structured, logical approach to problem solving. For example, I won first place in the engineering category of my high school's annual science fair. In my project, I researched over a hundred building techniques and developed a system that delivers a 5% increase in weight bearing ability compared to today's most commonly used techniques for bridge building.

"As you can see on my resume, I also have experience in everything from developing improvements for construction techniques to creating engineering plans for dog kennels. I'm the treasurer for our university's physics club, which is helping me build my budgeting skills, and I'm a staff reporter for our school's newspaper, which helps me polish my writing skills.

"Now I'm looking for a position where I can apply my passion to solve even more complicated problems. That passion and my problem solving skills will make me a great choice for this job."

Write your answer to this question here.

PASSION: _____

_____

_____

EXPERIENCE: _____

_____

_____

_____

_____

_____

_____

_____

_____

_____

_____

NEXT: _____

_____

_____

_____

_____

Opening Question #4:

Sample question: Why are you interested in this job?

Sample answer for someone seeking a computer industry job:

"I've always been passionate about diagnosing and fixing computer problems. From what I read in the job description for this position, it looks like you want someone who can diagnose issues and develop improvements for software programs. If I understand correctly, you also want someone who can resolve technical issues with computer networks. That's exactly the kind of work I love doing.

"For the past few summers, I've worked at a computer store coding and debugging software applications. I've also analyzed computer networks and installed improvements to make them run more effectively. As you can see from my resume, I've been able to find ways to reduce network downtimes by an average of 80%. I've also worked with customers to address their technical service requests, and I really enjoy this type of work.

"Now I'm looking for a job where I can work with employees to help them with their technical issues. I'm also looking for opportunities to train people to use their computers more effectively. My understanding is that you're looking for people to do that type of work. I'd like to be part of your company since you're offering the kind of work I enjoy most."

Write your answer to this question here.

PASSION: _____

_____

_____

EXPERIENCE: _____

_____

_____

_____

_____

_____

_____

_____

_____

_____

NEXT: _____

_____

_____

_____

_____

Opening Question #5:

Sample question: Why should I hire you?

Sample answer for someone seeking a teaching job:

"You should hire me because of my passion for working with kids. I also have the experience needed to demonstrate I can be effective at teaching.

"As you can see from my resume, I've spent two summers as a camp counselor. During that time, I've worked with over a hundred kids between the ages of ten and thirteen. My favorite part of that job was helping those kids improve their skills. My specialty was taking complicated tasks, like setting up an overnight campsite, and breaking it down into easy-to-understand steps. When I was hired to come back for my second summer, I was promoted to Senior Camp Counselor. I was given more responsibility and larger class sizes. In addition to teaching survival skills, I became the lead instructor for writing and crafts classes, and I coached several sports including basketball and soccer.

"As I said, I love working with kids, especially kids between the ages of ten and thirteen. Now I'm looking to start my career as a middle school teaching assistant or substitute teacher. You should hire me because I come with the passion and the experience you're looking for if you want someone who can connect with kids in this age range."

Write your answer to this question here.

PASSION: _____

_____

_____

EXPERIENCE: _____

_____

_____

_____

_____

_____

_____

_____

_____

_____

_____

NEXT: _____

_____

_____

_____

_____

Fit Question #1:

Sample question: What is your biggest strength?

Sample answer for someone seeking a marketing job:

"My biggest strength is my ability to identify opportunities that other people might miss. Let me give you an example from when I volunteered to be the webmaster for our university's running club. My task was to use our website to increase participation at our monthly fun runs.

"First, I did some research and learned that most students weren't even aware that we had a running club on campus, but they'd be interested in our fun runs if they knew about them ahead of time. Next, I created social media sites for our running club on Facebook, Instagram, and Twitter. Then, I posted weekly articles about the events on our social media feeds. Those articles drove traffic to our social media sites where students could sign up for our races.

"The result was a 300% increase in participation for our fun runs. I was able to get that result because I looked beyond our club's website and found opportunities to use social media to get some more people to our events."

Write your answer to this question here.

SITUATION: _____

_____

TASK: _____

_____

ACTIONS: _____

_____

_____

_____

_____

_____

_____

_____

_____

_____

_____

RESULT: _____

_____

_____

Fit Question #2:

Sample question: What is your biggest weakness?

Sample answer for someone seeking a nursing job:

"I'd say my biggest weakness has been my hesitancy to be assertive. I have a diplomatic style, and I'm working on being more assertive when needed. Let me give you an example from when I was an orderly at the Pleasanton Retirement Home. One of my tasks was to transition patients from a common area to their rooms at the end of each day.

"One time, there was an elderly woman who wasn't willing to leave the common area. I tried every diplomatic approach I could think of to coax her to her room. Nothing worked. Finally, another orderly came in and firmly told the woman that she had to go to her room or she'd lose the privilege of coming to the common area the next day. I originally thought that threatening a resident like that might seem rude, but it worked in that situation.

"As a result, I've learned to be more assertive when needed. I still start with a diplomatic approach, but I'm more willing to become assertive if the situation calls for it."

Note: This is a difficult question to answer. I recommend you choose a weakness that's not a deal-breaker in your career field. Since nurses should be very diplomatic, this answer is a good one. She also does a great job of explaining how she's working to overcome that weakness.

AMAZING JOB SEARCH GAMEPLAN

Write your answer to this question here.

SITUATION: _____

_____

TASK: _____

_____

ACTIONS: _____

_____

_____

_____

_____

_____

_____

_____

_____

_____

RESULT: _____

_____

_____

Fit Question #3:

Sample question: Can you tell me about a time when you demonstrated creativity?

Sample answer for someone seeking an engineering job:

"Last summer, I was an assistant office manager at an animal shelter. My task was to find a way to increase the number of dogs we could keep in our kennel building.

"I started by researching places where populations were becoming more dense. I noticed that in cities, people often lived in high-rise buildings, and they often lived with multiple people in small apartments. I decided to apply those lessons to our dog kennels. I designed kennels that could be stacked on top of each other so we could fit more kennels in the same space. I also researched which dog breeds and genders were most likely to coexist peacefully in the same living space. I built prototype kennel-apartments and tested them with a variety of dogs. After weeks of testing, I made adjustments to the designs, and I supervised a contractor who converted all our small-dog kennels to my new apartment-style design.

"Because I found a creative solution, the result was a 40% increase in the number of dogs that could be housed in our kennel building. As an added benefit, I discovered that the dogs that moved in with roommates were less aggressive and more playful. We noticed that those dogs were 10% more likely to get adopted because their behavior appealed to people who came to our facility looking to find a pet."

Write your answer to this question here.

SITUATION: _____

_____

TASK: _____

_____

ACTIONS: _____

_____

_____

_____

_____

_____

_____

_____

_____

_____

RESULT: _____

_____

_____

Fit Question #4:

Sample question: Can you tell me about a time when you used your analytical skills?

Sample answer for someone seeking a computer industry job:

"When I was in high school, I was working to get my Eagle Scout certification. For my final project, I chose to design and install a new computer network for my high school. I chose that project because of my passion for computers and because our school's network was frequently going down.

"I started by calculating the data usage for the existing network. I learned that our bandwidth usage was 50% higher than other high school of similar size. I also learned that our usage had doubled every year for the past five years. Then, I projected the bandwidth needs for the next five years and determined how much the network would need to expand over time. I used that information to design a network that could handle the current usage needs and be expandable to handle future needs. Since we only needed the bandwidth from 8:00 a.m. to 5:00 p.m. on weekdays, I researched other places that could use our network during our downtimes. I found a nearby university that was willing to buy our available bandwidth on evenings and weekends.

"As a result, I designed and installed a new network that reduced downtime by 97% over the next three years. Plus, that network cost 40% less than the network our school district's IT department originally recommended."

Write your answer to this question here.

SITUATION: _____

_____

TASK: _____

_____

ACTIONS: _____

_____

_____

_____

_____

_____

_____

_____

_____

_____

_____

RESULT: _____

_____

_____

Fit Question #5:

Sample question: Can you tell me about a time when you demonstrated persistence?

Sample answer for someone seeking a teaching job:

"I'm a volunteer basketball coach for the Boys & Girls Club. My main task is to teach kids to work tougher in teams. That was particularly difficult last year when I had a few boys who really didn't get along with each other.

"I tried everything I could find in coaching manuals and books about teamwork. I tried to define shared goals, create a culture of cooperation, and open up lines of communication. Nothing worked. Two of the boys were particularly challenging as they fought during nearly every practice. Finally, I got their parents' permission to take those two boys on a field trip together. We went on an eight-hour hike, which was grueling. Near the end of the hike, they finally let down their guards and started talking to each other. They learned that they had some similar interests. They even exchanged phone numbers at the end of the day.

"As a result of my persistence, those two boys have become best friends. Because I wouldn't give up on them, they've learned to work together, and they've become two of the best players on a winning basketball team."

Write your answer to this question here.

SITUATION: _____

_____

TASK: _____

_____

ACTIONS: _____

_____

_____

_____

_____

_____

_____

_____

_____

_____

RESULT: _____

_____

_____

Case Question #1:

Sample question: If your brand's sales start to decline, what would you do?

Sample answer for someone seeking a marketing job:

"I'd start with the 3C's, and then I'd move on to the 4P's.

"First, I'd start with my customers. Have there been any changes in their purchasing behavior or their preferences that are impacting my sales? Then, I'd look at competitors. Have any of them launched any new products or changed their promotional strategies recently? Next, I'd look at my company. Have we changed the way we've prioritized our brands or have we reallocated resources across our initiatives?

"Then, I'd look at the 4P's. Have my products changed in any way? For example, did I reformulate anything? Next, I'd ask if I changed my pricing strategy. Am I charging more for my products than I used to? Then, I'd look at my promotions. Have I changed my marketing message or tactics recently? Finally, I'd look at the placement of my products. Have I lost distribution, or am I losing shelf space in stores?

"Once I asked those questions, I'd assess what's happening to cause my brand's sales to decline. Then, I'd formulate a strategy to get my brand back on track."

Write your answer to this question here.

FRAMEWORK: _____

_____

ANSWER: _____

_____

_____

_____

_____

_____

_____

_____

_____

_____

_____

_____

_____

_____

_____

_____

_____

_____

Case Question #2:

Sample question: If you had a patient who fainted, what would you do?

Sample answer for someone seeking a nursing job:

"For fainting, I'd use a mnemonic called L.A.R.C.

"First, I'd lay the person flat on their back. That's the L. Then, I'd check their airway, which is the A. If they weren't breathing, I'd administer CPR. Next, I'd try to revive them, which is the R. I could do that by tapping on their arm and talking to them loudly. If that didn't work, I'd call for help. That's the C.

"If at any time, they started to vomit, I'd turn them onto their side, so they don't swallow the vomit. If they regained consciousness, I would check to see if they might be dehydrated or if they might not have eaten in a while. If that were the case, I might try to get them to drink some water or some juice.

"Finally, I'd stay with them, until they were fully recovered or until help arrived."

Write your answer to this question here.

FRAMEWORK: _____

_____

ANSWER: _____

_____

_____

_____

_____

_____

_____

_____

_____

_____

_____

_____

_____

_____

_____

_____

_____

Case Question #3:

Sample question: If I asked you to design a new highway intersection, how would you approach that?

Sample answer for someone seeking an engineering job:

"I'd use a process called SOLVE. It stands for Study the problem, Organize the facts, Line up the plan, Verify the plan, and Examine the answer.

"Here's how it works. First, I'd study the intersection to find any issues or opportunities for improving it. Then, I'd organize facts, like how much space I had to work with, how the traffic currently flowed through the intersection, and what the future needs might be. Then, I'd line up a plan, which could involve designing the number of lanes and whether stoplights might be needed. Then, I'd verify the plan by calculating whether my new design would improve the traffic flow. Finally, I'd examine my answer to make sure my assumptions and calculations were correct. Once I did all that, I'd show my plan to a few traffic experts to see if they could find any ways to improve it."

Write your answer to this question here.

FRAMEWORK: _____

_____

ANSWER: _____

_____

_____

_____

_____

_____

_____

_____

_____

_____

_____

_____

_____

_____

_____

_____

_____

Case Question #4:

Sample question: If your boss asked you to debug a computer program, how would you approach that?

Sample answer for someone seeking a computer industry job:

"I'd use a process that I call re-scuffed. It stands for Recognize that a bug exists, find the Source of the bug, identify the Cause, determine the Fix, and Test the fix.

"Recognizing that a bug exists would be the easy part, since my boss has asked me to fix it. To find the source, I'd test the program to see where it stops working and when the bug occurs. Then, I'd find the cause of the bug by going into the source code to see where the program might be faulty. Then, I'd determine the fix by writing updated source code that is bug-free. Finally, I'd test the fix by rerunning the program after I inserted the new code. If everything works, then I would have successfully debugged the program. If not, I'd go back to the beginning and do the re-scuffed process again until I fixed the error."

Write your answer to this question here.

FRAMEWORK: _____

_____

ANSWER: _____

_____

_____

_____

_____

_____

_____

_____

_____

_____

_____

_____

_____

_____

_____

_____

_____

_____

Case Question #5:

Sample question: How would you handle a parent who wants constant updates on their child's progress?

Sample answer for someone seeking a teaching job:

"I'd use a technique called ASKE, which is spelled A.S.K.E. The A stands for Assume positive intent. S is for Seek to understand. K means Keep looking for an acceptable solution, and E means Elevate when needed.

"I'd start by assuming that the parent has positive intentions. They might want to ensure that their child is getting a good education and making the progress that they should be making. Next, I'd seek to understand why the parent wanted such frequent updates. I'd meet with the parents and ask them about any concerns they may have. Then, I'd keep working with them to find an acceptable solution. I'd reassure the parents about our teaching techniques and their child's progress. I'd also see if there was a way I could update them frequently enough to meet their needs, without it becoming unreasonable for their child or for me. If the issue continued, I'd elevate the issue by getting input from other teachers who have more experience than I have. If necessary, I might even elevate the issue to the school's principal to see if he/she had any suggestions."

Write your answer to this question here.

FRAMEWORK: _____

_____

ANSWER: _____

_____

_____

_____

_____

_____

_____

_____

_____

_____

_____

_____

_____

_____

_____

_____

_____

SAMPLE INTERVIEW ANSWERS

Interview Checklist

INTERVIEW CHECKLIST

Interview Checklist

Things to bring to your interview:

____ A handbag or briefcase (big enough to fit the following)

____ A nice folder with a notepad

____ Ten copies of your resume

____ Five copies of your references list

____ A list of questions you might want to ask an interviewer

____ A pen

____ Two or three small bags of snacks (nuts, granola bars, etc.)

____ A bottle of water

____ Breath mints

Things to do the week before your interview:

____ Make sure your interview clothes are clean and pressed

____ Make sure your interview shoes are polished

____ Research the company

____ Practice your P-E-N, S-T-A-R, and case question answers

INTERVIEW CHECKLIST

Things to do the day before your interview:

____ Double-check that your clothes and shoes are in good shape

____ Pack your handbag or briefcase with the items listed above

____ Practice your P-E-N, S-T-A-R, and case question answers one last time

____ Get a good night's rest

Things to do the day of your interview:

____ Wake up early

____ Eat a big, healthy breakfast

____ Check the weather to see if you need an umbrella

____ Check traffic to ensure you don't need to leave extra early

____ Arrive thirty minutes early

____ When you arrive, find a restroom. Use it and check your appearance

____ Check in with the receptionist at least ten minutes before your interview time

Things to do during your interview:

_____ Greet the interviewer with a friendly smile and a firm handshake

_____ Nail the interview! This should be easy, given all the preparation you've done

_____ At the end of the interview, thank the recruiter and tell them how interested you are in the job

_____ Follow up with a short, polite email to the recruiter, thanking him/her and reiterating your interest in the job

ABOUT THE AUTHOR

About the Author

Richard Blazevich has led the campus recruiting efforts for the marketing department of a multinational consumer products company. Over the years, he has interviewed hundreds of candidates for a wide variety of roles. He has also led interview workshops for career development offices and student organizations at some of the top universities in the United States.

Richard is a senior director of marketing with over fifteen years of experience. He received an MBA with an emphasis in Marketing and Business Strategy from the University of Michigan and a Bachelor's degree in Business from Montana State University.

If you've enjoyed this book, here are other books by this author that you might want to read.

Amazing Job Search Gameplan: College Student Addition

This book is designed to help college students get their first big job. It provides an easy-to-follow plan for researching companies, perfecting resumes, and nailing job interviews. You get advice for using tools that are easily available on college campuses to help students be successful in a competitive job market.

Amazing Interview Answers

In this book, you'll find a list of 44 common interview questions along with winning answers for each question. You'll also get frameworks for preparing your interview answers and tips for researching jobs.

If you're the type of person who learns by example, this book is for you.

That's a Bullseye

Find out what happens to Lisa Brimmer after she joins the Premier Sporting Goods company. *That's a Bullseye* picks up the story as Lisa works to turn around a struggling company. This book is for anyone interested in marketing. It provides a practical approach for creating your marketing strategy and growing your business in an ever-changing environment.